An Outrageous Commitment

FEB

2009

CO

Also by Dr. Ronn Elmore

How to Love a Black Man

How to Love a Black Woman

An Outrageous Commitment

The 48 Vows of an Indestructible Marriage

Ronn Elmore, Psy.D.

HarperResource

An imprint of HarperCollins*Publishers*

AN OUTRAGEOUS COMMITMENT. Copyright © 2003 by Dr. Ronn Elmore.
All rights reserved. Printed in the United States of America.
No part of this book may be used or reproduced in any manner whatsoever
without written permission except in the case of brief quotations
embodied in critical articles and reviews. For information address
HarperCollins Publishers Inc., 10 East 53rd Street, New York, NY 10022.

HarperCollins books may be purchased for educational, business,
or sales promotional use. For information please write:
Special Markets Department, HarperCollins Publishers Inc.,
10 East 53rd Street, New York, NY 10022.

First HarperResource paperback edition published 2004

Designed by Oksana Kushnir

The Library of Congress has catalogued the hardcover edition as follows:

Elmore, Ronn.
An outrageous commitment : the 48 vows of an indestructible marriage /
Ronn Elmore.—1st. ed.
p. cm.
ISBN 0-06-093620-7 (pbk.)
ISBN 0-06-621130-1
1. Communication in marriage.   2. Interpersonal communication.
3. Marriage—Religious aspects.   I. Title.
HQ734 .E553 2003
646.7'8—dc21   2002192214

06 07 08 RRD 10 9 8 7 6 5 4 3

To the Lord Jesus Christ,
and to Aladrian,
both of whom continue to love me
with a truly outrageous commitment

Contents

A Note to the Reader

Throughout this book only the author's and his wife's real name appear; all others, aside from Julia Roberts, have been changed. Also, license has been taken with certain narrative details for illustrative purposes and to maintain the subjects' privacy.

The Adam and Eve vignettes that introduce each chapter are parables. They were created to help us reflect more deeply on our own marriages and identify the real-life opportunities we have to live these vows of unconditional commitment. The parables are *not* derived from biblical accounts.

Preface

An Outrageous Commitment: *The 48 Vows of an Indestructible Marriage* is about making extraordinary choices that can increase the quality, durability, and longevity of your marriage. These uncommon commitments transcend the sentimental declarations we all make on our wedding day. Should you choose to enact these vows, expect to be challenged beyond your natural capacities and rewarded beyond your loftiest expectations.

Within these pages you will have an encounter, perhaps a life-changing one, with the unspoken, overlooked, or previously unknown vows of a marriage that can "take it." No matter what *it* may be. Virtually all of the practical, spiritual principles you will find here can be applied to any marriage. Starting today. In spite of what has or has not happened in the past. Even if only one of you is ready to act on them.

Making the choice to give your love away freely, unconditionally, self-sacrificially—forever—is extraordinary, to say the least. Making and keeping that choice again and again, day after day, is nothing short of miraculous.

This book is an invitation to perform miracles.

Introduction

Anyone who has been married for more than five minutes realizes that it takes so much more than we were ever told. More than love. More than sincerity. More than compatibility, know-how, good communication skills, or hard effort. More than healthy self-esteem or good upbringing. More than a romantic nature, a willingness to listen, or megadoses of "quality time." These alone will eventually prove inadequate to bind one imperfect person to another, forever.

As a longtime couples' therapist, a minister, and a husband, I am well aware that *commitment* is an overworked term these days. Sadly, it has lost much of its gritty strength and become a warm, fuzzy abstraction that makes few concrete demands of anyone. Once, the word was understood to mean the whole weighty bundle of spiritual, physical, emotional, and material obligations we make to each other in marriage. Now it often only seems to mean what we hope to *feel*. Or the good we *intend* to do for each other—*if* all goes as planned. Of course, in marriage, next to nothing goes exactly as planned.

Our commitment is repeatedly challenged by the fierce and relentless enemies of our unions: unfulfilled expectations, mismatched interests, previously undetected sensitivities, unanticipated crises, anger, restlessness, and fatigue.

For over fifteen years I have worked with hundreds of apparently sincere husbands and wives. As they stare back at me from the couch, I always wonder whether they will be one of the rare couples who will rise above the inevitable bumps and bruises of married life, or who will eventually be brought to the point of collapse by them. At times, over the course of more than twenty years, I have looked at my own marriage and wondered the same thing.

When we first met, Aladrian was a nineteen-year-old college student, the privileged only child of her God-fearing parents. Upon the sober-minded counsel of her father, she was pursuing an undergraduate degree in economics at a prestigious Los Angeles–area college. Her true passion, however, was singing. She aspired to a career in opera. Aladrian was working her way through college by playing the piano and directing the choir at a large local church. Freshly transplanted from New York, I had begun attending that same church.

Aladrian was a bubbly and outgoing coed. I was a world-weary and slightly cynical twenty-two-year-old who had grown bored and impatient with small-town life and left home at seventeen to pursue a career as a professional dancer in New York. A few years later, having achieved a measure of success performing around the world, I landed in L.A. determined to become a star (and, as much, to avoid facing another East Coast winter).

Until we met that Sunday night when I heard Aladrian sing for the first time, neither of us had marriage in our immediate plans; but we were instantly smitten by each other. We fell in love with each other—and with the euphoria-producing feeling of being in love. Feeling the way we did, it was quite easy to talk and to listen to each other, to freely offer each other our care and affection, and to dream of spending our lives together in uninterrupted bliss.

On our second date we talked of marriage as if we had been seriously contemplating it for years. Neither of us knew everything there was to know about the other, but we were determined not to lose each other to anyone else. We fully expected that our as-yet unabated passion and euphoria was *the* "assurance" of the rightness of our becoming husband and wife.

We quickly gained the endorsement of our friends and family. Many gently warned us that "marriage is not as easy as it looks." Still, the unanimous consensus was *"If you're 'in love' with each other nothing else really matters."* We patiently endured their warnings and silently took pride in the fact that we were not only deeply in love, but ours felt unique, too sublime for us to ever have to face the kind of marital difficulties that others did. We were certain ours was, and ever would be, the love of all time. We could just feel it.

At least at first we did.

During the months leading up to the wedding, and shortly after it, we were powerfully confronted by the undeniable fact that our once-overflowing passion only sustained Aladrian and me when our marriage (and our mate) conformed to our naïve "happily married" ideal. At times when it didn't look or feel as it once had, we worried that we had "fallen out of love." Our attraction to, and "need" for, each other was waning and we didn't know what to do about it. Our feelings, the glue that had previously held us together, began to evaporate.

It was clear to us that if our relationship was to survive and endure we needed something stronger, something more dependable as its foundation. In our frustration we embarked, unsteadily at first, upon a spiritual adventure. We were desperate for God to make clear to us what the elements are that make a marriage work and last. Exactly what makes a marriage indestructible?

Life lessons on this order are often learned slowly and at the expense of our longest-held (but completely unrealistic) assumptions about the nature of lasting love. Our search led us to an appreciation of our variable mutual attraction, our fluctuating passions, but to no longer look to them as the defining elements of our love for each other. Our search eventually led us past exhilarating, but superficial and ultimately collapsible, *feelings* of love and into the farther reaches of unconditional commitment.

In loving each other we wanted (and at times still want) to set easy-to-manage limits as to how far this commitment had to go. Left to our own personal preferences, the limits of it would be just this side of *reasonable*, never across the far borders into *outrageous*. We reckoned, as does apparently an entire generation of husbands and wives, that having a solid marriage simply meant at times being willing to put up with some momentary inconveniences and challenging but quickly resolvable inequities. We were mistaken.

During the early days of our journey we made two stunning discoveries: (1) You cannot impose limits on how "unreasonable" are the self-sacrifices demanded by unconditional love and (2) you can't place limits on how long you will have to keep making those extraordinary self-sacrifices. These two facts are what make marriage an outrageous commitment.

It has been over two decades since we began, in desperation, asking God to help us undergird our marriage with something infinitely more profound and enduring than passion's dizzying roller-coaster ride. For over two-thirds of that time I have ministered to hundreds of other couples who also hunger for more; who hunger for the kind of marriage that is impervious to fluctuating feelings and circumstances. But how?

I am completely convinced that it is only possible by living the 48 vows you are about to encounter. The more of them you decide to incorporate into your marriage, the more likely you are to look back one day on what will have been a long and flourishing marriage.

Everyone stands ready to give advice about what keeps a marriage from going to the dogs. It is usually centered on outcomes. As in "If you do this or that thing, you're certain to get this glorious result." Or, "*Never* do that, or this very rotten thing will happen." We all know the rhetoric, the conventional how-tos, the dos and don'ts of a "happy marriage." They typically have to do with agreeing on the proper positioning of toilet seats and toothpaste tubes, or how to speak up or shut up, or how to share the money, the power, or the blame.

We've all read the books with the snappy titles and the money-back guarantee that their tips and techniques are sure to make your relationship altogether wonderful. (I've written some of them myself.) In spite of it all, marriages continue to crumble around us at an alarming rate. We have begun to sense that it must take something more than experts' sound bites to ensure an unshakable foundation of indestructibility in our marriages.

I have long suspected that our adoration of simple, energy-efficient tips and techniques is, in fact, rooted in self-interest. Mutual self-interest perhaps, but self-interest all the same. We crave surefire steps and strategies because more than wanting what is full of goodness, extravagant selflessness, and unconditional commitment, we simply want what's guaranteed to "work"—and with the least amount of time and effort expended. So both partners go to their respective drawing boards, devise their own personal definition of unconditional love and commitment, and move swiftly to enforce it as law upon their mates. Our mate's failure to comply with these self-centered whims (though they often sound so romantic, so spiritual) seems like justifiable grounds to repossess our wedding bands.

But for the rare few with marriages of increasing substance and enduring strength, at some point it became clear to me that marriage, in its highest and best sense, calls for a gradual (and ceaseless) emptying of our self-interest and a completely *unnatural* kind of self-sacrifice that simply makes no earthly sense—except in the context of matrimony. Therein is the element of the divine. It is in making and keeping these admittedly outrageous commitments to each other when we feel like it and when we don't. They are higher than our personal preferences. Higher than the tips and techniques of a "happy marriage." These are the defining vows of *holy* matrimony.

Should you decide to make and keep the commitments I will introduce here, be prepared to be called either a miracle worker or a fool. At times you will consider yourself one or the other. A miracle worker because you will see yourself giving, taking, accepting, and benefiting from the unique sacrifices of outrageous commitment and you'll know, beyond a shadow of a doubt, that you could not have done it on your own. At other times, you'll suspect yourself of being foolish for having let so much get away from you when there appears to be so little return on your extravagant investment. It is only by just this kind of "foolish" behavior that you can build (or rebuild) a marriage that cannot be toppled over by any kind of adversity.

You are likely to detect right away that this book is quite different from any book you've ever read about marriage. Each chapter includes words of instruction and encouragement as might be spoken by God Himself: wise but gentle and intimate, challenging and affirming, insistent, yet patient, instructive, sometimes playful, and at all times inspiring. You'll get the most benefit from it if, as you read, you try to imagine that it's God speaking directly to you, revealing or redefining the most vital commitments of marriage, and pointing out the daily opportunity you have to live them out—and benefit from them—in your marriage.

We all have our own widely differing opinions about who God is. For those expecting theological debate or mystical teachings that are confusing to the uninitiated, you won't find it here. Truth that cannot be plainly worded should be considered suspect.

The two points with which we all seem to agree are that *God is love* and *God is truth*. Or at the very least, *God is infinitely loving*, and *God is absolutely truthful*. That being so, it is reasonable to expect that God is qualified to speak credibly to you, and to all of us, about uncommon commitments of marriage.

But I must warn you of two potential dangers that could keep you from getting the benefits of this book:

- Taking issue with the spiritual nature of the message and missing out on the practical principles ahead that can revolutionize your marriage, or
- Becoming so fascinated with the practical insights that you fail to see beyond them to the real Person who loves you with absolutely boundless commitment and wants you to know how to offer that unique love in your marriage.

We tend to want to reduce spiritual principles down to predictable formulas and oversimplified lists of dos and don'ts. Or, as bad, we tend to "overspiritualize" the practical application, perhaps to render it so otherworldly and complex as to excuse ourselves from having to do it.

Of course commitment is an issue of practical concerns, but to overlook its profoundly spiritual nature is to hover on the surface and never plumb its depths.

If you will keep your mind, your heart, and this book open, you will have an indescribable encounter here with what love in marriage really looks like and acts like. What it sacrifices, what it endures, and to what it aspires. And the ways it can both humble and elevate you and your relationship.

For the next 234 pages, imagine that you have arrived at a divine appointment with the ultimate marriage counselor. The One who came up with the idea of divinely self-sacrificing, increasingly intimate, joyous, and enduring marriage in the first place. Such an approach can turn reading this book into a spiritual adventure where limitless possibilities exist to enrich—or completely transform—your marriage.

That brings us three very valid questions you are likely to be considering at this moment:

- *Could there really be something more to establishing a rock-solid marriage than fate, passion, and surefire techniques?*
- *Can it possibly make any measurable difference in my marriage?*
- *Will I actually be able to do what it takes to achieve that difference?*

There is. It can. You will.

It is better not to vow
than to make a vow
and not fulfill it.

—Ecclesiastes 5:5

The Vow of Outrageous Commitment

In marriage, your self-sacrifice will not always be noticed, appreciated, or reciprocated; but it has the power to disarm our natural tendency toward passionate self-centeredness.

T

O BE TRUTHFUL, I thought it would be different from this," said The Woman. She had risked hurting Adam by saying so, but this was too important to lie about. "So you are disappointed?" The Man asked, after several seconds of silence. "A bit, I suppose. Aren't you?" continued Eve. Adam's face always spoke plainly, even when his words failed him. Eve could not help but say what had been occupying her thoughts for so long. "Did you expect that we'd have to work so hard at this? Or that we could love each other and still find it so difficult to understand each other? It's just not as I thought it would be." Adam felt the same way, and for several minutes debated with himself as to whether he should admit it or not. Neither of them noticed the light mist that had descended upon Eden until, with a sudden clap of thunder, it became a late summer downpour. The two moved hurriedly indoors. As they entered, both immediately caught sight of The Creator, who beckoned them to join Him. The Man and The Woman sat down by the blazing fire He had built to warm them, and by which He would teach them about The Vow of Outrageous Commitment.

It is no secret that marriage is a most outrageous commitment. Outrageous because for it to be the glorious thing that I intended, you must offer another person what simply makes no earthly sense. Marriage challenges you to make and keep vows that don't always seem fair or advantageous—or even possible. More than promises, they are solemn vows made by mere mortals who, on their own, do not possess the power to keep them. Promises are only expressions of what one sincerely intends to do or be, or give, up to the finite limits of his or her human abilities. Vows speak of what you will do up to the limits of My ability.

*There are no limits to My ability. I have simply decided to love you, with
no conditions, no rational explanations, no reservations. Love as I love,
with the steady undeterred force of outrageous commitment.*

We label something outrageous when its benefits aren't plainly in
view but we are called upon to do it anyway. Unconditional love
seems outrageous to us when the object of that commitment has by
no means earned it, or when it demands more of our most cherished
personal resources than we are willing to dispense. Something as
slight as a kiss can seem like an outrageous offer after our mate has
broken a promise, or nursed a grudge, or ignored a request we've
made. Somehow we've come to believe that love is a finite, irreplace-
able commodity that we could use up, stock, and reserve.

Still, our souls desire something this high and pure; something
that makes ordinary marriages extraordinary, struggling marriages as
solid as granite, and dead marriages resurrected to new life. In spite
of all our best arguments against it, self-sacrifice is the facet of love
that most reflects the height, the depth, the width, and the breadth
of God's love for you.

Along with many qualities that I loved about my wife, Aladrian,
there were others that I soon discovered were not to my liking. In spite
of my most earnest efforts to change her to fit my expectations, she
persisted in being genuinely herself. In those early days, suddenly
being married and living life in full, constant view of someone else was
especially traumatic to her. She was often moody, prone to depression,
and struggling to set personal goals and pursue them confidently.

I valued cool, unemotional determination and sure-footed decisiveness. She struck me as self-indulgent and timid—qualities I
abhorred. I offered Aladrian *reasonable* amounts of sympathy and
good advice and expected change to be soon coming. It was not.

She found me disappointingly unfeeling and marked by the kind of hyper-self-sufficiency and independence that suggested I didn't need anybody—including my wife—for anything. She made it clear to me that what she really needed from me was not another day of my patronizing advice and pity. She needed me to halt what she termed my "cold, clinical analysis" of her and my pained facial expressions that vividly portrayed contempt. She wanted me to make the commitment to treat her as if it mattered to me that she was there. To hold her close, literally and figuratively, but to keep all of my diagnoses to myself. *Outrageous!*

Outrageous commitment, and the self-sacrificing acts that demonstrate it, are hard to explain, let alone defend. It is lavish, unearned, often unappreciated, and not always reciprocated. Sacrificing our own interests for the sake of another person disarms our natural human tendency toward passionate self-centeredness. Making lofty vows to each other takes little effort. Keeping them, however, will take all your strength and much more besides. It is not to be accomplished by mere habits, or well-kept rules, but by your willing embrace of selfless sacrifice.

You may have demonstrated outrageous commitment and not known it. Wherever it exists it will show itself in abundantly practical, observable ways like:

- waking up each morning and deciding, yet again, to offer your best today—in spite of what happened yesterday;
- deciding to keep talking about and planning for your future together, even when the present is troubling;
- delaying (or sacrificing altogether) the night out, the exotic vacation, the new car, or any long-awaited pleasure, because you need to take a loss this time so that your mate can gain something infinitely more valuable;

- giving the one you love the space to show he or she is profoundly human, but not in danger of losing your devotion because of it. Or, in my case,
- making my feelings known to my wife, but investing the extra time and effort to make my desires sound like requests, not demands.

It is in making and keeping vows like these and the ones you are about to encounter in the pages ahead that transcend mere marriage and establish *holy matrimony*.

Is your brand of commitment to your mate and your marriage visible and practical, or merely verbalized and well intended?

The Vow of Mutual Submission

Submission doesn't mean allowing yourself to be dominated. It means you willingly choose to yield, voluntarily adjusting yourself to the altogether unique mate you have chosen.

THEY STOOD BEFORE HIM, like two petulant children, each wholly determined to level the other's protest. "The word is *helpmate*, Eve! It means you are to do what I ask. That's why you are here." "Wrong, Adam! I am your wife, not your slave," countered Eve. God waited in silence for one of them to seek His counsel. Neither of them even looked His way. Adam had demanded his dinner one too many times. This time she had "served" him by dumping a steaming pot of curried stew at his feet. Then she counted the seconds until he began his inevitable tirade on the topic of *submission*. As usual they both had much to say. And, as usual, they would have exhausted each other with their opinions, except The One who had joined them together abruptly stepped between them, silencing the debate, to once again clarify The Vow of Mutual Submission.

It is the very thought of bowing down that makes you cringe. You, and all the generations of spouses who will come after you, have an innate disdain for anything even faintly resembling dominance by one of you and subservience by the other. So do I. Submission—mutual submission—is something altogether different from that. Nothing about it calls for one of you to bow down and the other to be the one who gets bowed down to. To submit is to make a bold yet humbling choice to mold all that you are, all that you possess and control, into the shape of what meets your beloved's needs. I am counting on both of you to model it in its purest form so that others do not distort it due to their faulty assumption about its meaning. Submission is love's ultimate act, because it is love given over to someone's benefit more than, and at times, instead of, your own.

As both a minister and a marriage counselor, I have found that there is nothing more controversial between modern-day spouses than the notion of submission in marriage. I wish I had a dollar for every time I've heard a man or woman in premarital counseling groan in disgust at the very mention of the word. Or when a bride (almost always the bride) repeatedly seeks reassurances that I will not include "the S word" in their wedding ceremony. Or the ones who now resolutely declare to me that they have made peace with the once off-putting idea of submission and are ready to meekly defer to their husband's every decision. Though they sound determined, they always look as if they'd just said "yes" to cutting off their own arms and legs.

Clearly submission in marriage is either the most *demeaning*, or the most *misunderstood* concept of them all.

Submission does not mean voluntarily allowing yourself to be dominated by anyone. It means the willingness to yield. Obedience is rooted in one having more right and authority than another, including the right to demand the other's strict compliance, whether that person likes it or not. Submission, by contrast, is rooted in the idea of *choosing* to exercise your rights—or to voluntarily defer them—in a way that complements the unique needs and qualities of the mate you chose to marry. Not to reaffirm you own status or cash in on perceived privileges of your gender or any other personal distinctiveness.

The concept of submission has become so maligned and distorted that we instinctively run from it. In our swift retreat we never lay hold to the benefits of it. We see submission as denial of our rights rather than the exercise of them.

In a marriage, it is *mutual* submission that should be your aim. How you model it will influence how your children and their children will understand and apply it. It will not be the words and phrases that proceed from your mouth on the subject, but the way in which you are constantly seen intentionally and self-sacrificially yielding to each other's unique way of being.

You are not to defer to each other merely to make it possible for you to get your mate to cooperate with your every whim. It is not yielding to each other's selfish desires and arbitrary preferences that has the mark of extraordinary commitment upon it. Rather, it is the bold willingness to fashion your words, your will, your personal rights and self-interest, your available options and enticing opportunities—your very life—to conform with what is highest and best for your mate. Even though you will always have the right to do what serves your personal interests best, it is choosing to esteem your mate higher than yourself.

Under the stress of a dispute between us, Aladrian is much more emotionally expressive than I. Though it is not at all her way, she allows me to ask "just the facts" type questions and she answers them even though she'd prefer to stay for a time in the sheer emotion mode without having to respond to my interrogation. In this way she submits to my way, recognizing that after I "get it" intellectually I can serve her with my very best sensitivity and support. By submitting to my natural style in this way she powerfully contributes to getting the best of me. We both benefit.

At other times I submit to her natural style of communication in conflict that can include exaggeration, much detail, an evolving story line that comes out in slow, unwieldy pieces. I find that I do possess the ability—though not always the inclination—to wait, to listen, to tolerate my brain's going unsatisfied for a time, while I make my compassion and receptivity available to her. She is enriched. I am enriched. Mutual submission makes for mutual benefit.

Be careful that you do not allow the standards, values, and practices of most people to overshadow your commitment to mutual submission in your marriage. Look around; it is quite clear that it has not served them very well. They have marriages based upon forceful demands, unspoken threats, and manipulative power plays. These exist wherever one of you has more rights or authority; and the other one only has what has been given to them from that one. It forfeits any possibility of intimacy. Neither males nor females desire to give themselves over to vulnerable, self-disclosing intimacy with someone who believes she or he has the right to force the expressions of that devotion.

Submission is among the more challenging and controversial of all the vows. Your marriage can survive without it. Many do; but they do not—indeed cannot—flourish. It is in an environment of mutual submission that mates vividly demonstrate to each other the high value they place on each other.

Submission is always a choice. Where there is no choice, there is only the sense of obligation prompted by some form of being dominated and losing yourself in the process. Submission that does not originate from a willing heart will inevitably descend into resentment that inhibits any possibility of enduring intimacy and affection.

When submission proceeds from the powerful thrust of your willing decision it becomes the gracious offering that honors the one you love. Those who are recipients of it rise to new levels of honorable conduct themselves.

Are you more willing or less willing to practice submission in your marriage than you are in other significant relationships (e.g., with your parents, coworkers, children, or friends)?

The Vow of Exclusivity

An intimate marriage calls for the element of restriction, meaning some of your commitments must solely and exclusively be offered to your mate and no one else.

IT HAD TAKEN HER breath away. Eve had not known that she was capable of feeling this outraged and embarrassed. For several minutes now she had felt sick to her stomach, disoriented, and not sure her legs would go on holding her up. She was certain it was the mounting force of her anger that kept her from collapsing. Now Eve wanted—no, needed—to spew forth her outrage in one volcanic eruption upon Adam. She had been watching her husband for what seemed like an eternity, incredulous, as he conversed with the beautiful woman who sold cloth at the marketplace. The woman at whom all the men gawked the moment she arrived in the square. Though many others stood about talking in small groups around them, the quiet intensity of Adam and the merchant woman's conversation discouraged any interruption. If that were not enough, Adam put his hand up as if to shield his words from others' hearing, to offer them to her alone. Then, she and Adam simultaneously threw back their heads and laughed loudly. It was the deep, uninhibited laughter of those who had shared a secret to which no one else was privy. That did it. Just as Eve started her angry advance across the square toward Adam, alternately eyeing his throat and the merchant woman's, The Creator came into her view. Suddenly there in the public square, just seconds before teeming with people, there was no one but Adam and Eve, and He who would explain to them The Vow of Exclusivity.

At times you both give too much of your time and attentions away to those to whom you do not belong. You call it generosity, I call it robbery. By virtue of your intimate relationship there are certain treasures that you must reserve for each other, to the exclusion of all others. I have bound Myself—happily so—to a covenant of exclusivity with you.

Exclusivity in your covenant relationship with each other behaves no differently. Mind that you do not give away to others what you have already pledged to each other alone.

"Setting boundaries" is a pop-psychology catchphrase that is often used to describe one of the most important elements of marital commitment. The principle of *setting boundaries* is probably exactly what my grandmother meant when she warned each of her grandsons, when we married, that "From now on, there are some things you just don't ever take away from home."

To be married means that there are certain things that you reserve for each other—and only each other—even though there are others who want them from you. Even though you feel you have more than enough to share some of it with your mate and others as well. Marriage is an intimate, supremely self-sacrificing agreement between two parties that is entered into by choice, never obligation. Undying commitment, discipline, and lavish mutual regard are the hallmarks of a covenant relationship. But implicit in covenant is the often overlooked and underappreciated element of *exclusivity*.

By definition *exclusivity* deliberately calls for the element of restriction in your intimate marriage relationship. It means some commitments therein are made available only to your covenant partner and to no one else. When covenant commitments are made available to anyone else, it is robbery of what you have already pledged to your mate alone.

Though marriage is a covenant of exclusivity, human nature always yearns to include more, wanting to leave out nothing or no one. Too often, husbands and wives choose to share with others what must never be shared. The intimacy of physical or emotional nakedness, vowed exclusively to a spouse, is granted to assorted others or never fully reclaimed from past associations. They will generously offer the unrestricted availability of their time to a former lover, a new friend, to parents, to their livelihoods, or their pleasures while their mates live on the crumbs of what remains. Or they will earnestly go on acting as protector and provider for someone other than their covenant partner. The world is in grave need of an example of the vow of exclusivity that goes beyond mere words. You are to be a living, breathing promise, a visible pattern for others to follow. The commitments of your marriage must not be broken into portions and dispensed far and wide. They are to remain undivided, undiluted. To fail in that is to compromise the purity of covenant relationship.

It means nothing to claim your spouse as your beloved but remain unwilling to alter your other relationships in a way that proves it. Maintaining exclusivity is a covenant that involves keeping the "yes" of your vows by becoming comfortable saying "no" to your other competing alliances when need be. You must not fear saying to someone you love, appreciate, or owe, "Sorry, what you are seeking from me is something I cannot offer you." But where you have not revised your old alliances to fit your new covenant you are saying "no" to your new covenant to serve your old alliances. They are not equal commitments. And though you may declare you know that, do you demonstrate it daily by the commitments you prioritize highest and the ones you don't?

We live in a neighborhood where every homeowner must abide by our "Covenants, Conditions, and Restrictions." It is a set of detailed guidelines governing everything from what colors you may paint your own home to how many cars can be parked in your own driveway at any given time. Like all our neighbors we couldn't have moved in without pledging to submit ourselves to these restrictive commitments.

I have been known to raise the argument that the CC &R's limit individual freedoms and make us feel forced to comply in order to

satisfy someone else's wishes. Then I remember that we all voluntarily bound ourselves to the covenants and that if we are willing to yield
to the restrictions we are helping to maintain the quality and multiply
the value of our homes. Keeping the covenant commitments in marriage works by the same principle.

No longer insist upon the right to continue in secretive, soul-
baring conversations with a former mate. Never let secrets that your
partner shared with you privately be shared with anyone who may
think ill of your mate, or influence you to do so. It may seem obvious
that your body is exclusively your mate's, but consider the less obvious issue of exposing that body to others' eyes by the wearing of
provocative attire; or by an all-too-familiar flirtiness when you inter-
act with those of the opposite sex.

The reason covenants are so significant is not just because they
are such intimate promises, but they are all the more precious
because they are restricted to one's mate exclusively. Honoring such
promises of exclusivity allows for the possibility that you can indeed
trust that you may finally become naked and not ashamed, vulnerable, but unafraid.

**Does anyone else get more of the very best things
about you than your spouse?**

The Vow of Flexibility

The outrageous commitment to assume responsibilities and perform tasks that match neither your natural abilities nor your desires.

H E SUPPOSED THAT HE should be happy that his wife was with child. And he would have been on any day other than this one. It was near the end and Eve was having great difficulty getting around, so many of her chores fell to Adam. He had never worked so hard attempting tasks he had little experience doing. He had dropped the heavy stone mortar on his foot and burned his fingers making bread that tasted like sand. Today Adam had already made two trips to the river for water, both times spilling most of it on the way back. How did Eve balance the pots without losing even a drop? The Creator joined The Man on his third trip. "My son, how goes it with you on this exquisite day?" He asked. "I'd gladly trade the sunshine for some help with all this extra work. I am not suited for these kinds of chores," Adam glumly replied. "Is that so?" said The Creator. Then He relieved Adam of the water pot and answered the confused expression on his face by explaining to him The Vow of Flexibility.

You chafe against doing what you don't do best because it does not match the image of yourself that most appeals to you. In marriage your functions, responsibilities, and tasks are never set in stone. They must shift and change, for both of you, according to the present need and which of you is available to see to that need, at that time. Genuine love does not seek fulfillment of its self-image as its primary objective. Instead it is open to an infinite number of ways of expressing itself, whether it's a comfortable fit or a tedious one.

Your life together as husband and wife is not solely a bond of the spirit. It is also a functional alliance faced with countless chores and the daily obligation of seeing that they get done. The down-to-earth reality is that both of you will need to perform tasks and solve problems that match neither your natural abilities nor your desires. When they do not match your own, you should never assume that they match your mate's. Better that you are more concerned that the job gets done than with waging war (especially the silent but bitter kind) about which one of you "ought to" do it.

There is simply no way to see to everything—the bills, the children, the house, the car, the dishes, the laundry, the in-laws—to manage the mundane details of married life without making a sincere commitment to flexibility. It is the practical, unromantic commitment to submit yourself, at times, to managerial functions and responsibilities that you feel just "aren't me." They do not fit your schedule, your temperament, your personal strengths, or your hand-me-down notions of what's "men's work" and what's "women's work." With a steadfast commitment to the vow of flexibility anyone who eats may at times have to cook, the one who uses it will at times have to see to its repair, the one who spends will also have to reconcile the bank statements.

These tasks seldom require well-seasoned ability, passionate interest, or a particular gender to accomplish them. They just need one of you to get it done so that the two of you can move on to other, more complex (and more rewarding) relational "chores" that will always need your attention and efforts. A couple I once counseled complained with great frustration that they never seemed to have the time anymore for intimate conversations—or even for making love. We soon discovered that much of what was keeping them so busy was their long, daily debates over whose responsibility it was (and whose it wasn't) to have handled yet another household chore that didn't get done. For the "pleasure" of avoiding doing something that's "not my job" they were paying dearly. Once they recognized that their rigid inflexibility was making them lose out on too much romance they became models of flexibility.

No one argues about the *principle* of flexibility—it's the *practice* of it that we resist, sometimes because we despise the boring drudgery of a particular task. Or because we'd all much rather play to our strengths, delighting in the sense of competency and self-satisfaction of doing what we do well. At times we may also resist because of the competitive spirit lurking within and warning us not to perform a task that our mate does so much better than we do. Sometimes we are operating from someone's idea of who's supposed to do what, usually our peers, our parents, or other authority figures. People who don't live at your house. Who are not married to your mate. Who don't know beans about what it takes to manage the practical details that keep your home moving along efficiently. Your willingness to function flexibly is the key to productivity and fairness in your relationship.

The inflexible miss out on so many available possibilities. For them there is only one way to get a given job done—one person who's got to do it, and one who doesn't have to. Those marriage partners who are committed to fluid shifts and turns can get more done, with less drama. They are simply tasks, not places to prove our value and clout. One couple I counseled was driving each other crazy because she believed it was her sole responsibility to cook the meals, but he and the kids sometimes got hungry before she returned home from work. She insisted it was a matter of disrespect when she arrived home to find that her husband had already put together a meal and fed everyone. He, on the other hand, found it offensive when she researched a stock ("his job") and added a few shares to their portfolio. Instead of both of them enjoying meals sometimes that they didn't make, and both of them prospering from investments they didn't have to do the homework for, they argued about whose turf was whose. Flexible roles and responsibilities is a sure way to expand your repertoire of abilities. Quite likely you could do a previously unfamiliar or unwelcome task sufficiently well if you started doing it from time to time—not because you have to, but simply because once you do it, neither of you has to do it and both of you are then available to join each other doing something you love. At the very least you will give your mate some relief from having to do that one all the time, or you both reap the benefits of finding it getting done when it's gone undone so long because it's not on either of your lists.

Make an outrageous commitment to define practical resolutions about who does what with practical criteria: before you choose to do or refuse to do what you believe isn't your job, ask yourself:

1. Do I have the time? (Or can I make the time? Will it keep me from responsibly handling the tasks we've agreed are mine to do? If not, go ahead and do it.)
2. Do I have the ability (or can I gain the ability by trying it) to do this chore at least adequately, or to see that it gets done by someone who does?
3. Is it beneficial? Will it positively contribute to my mate or my marriage for me to do this or will it accommodate my mate's irresponsibility?

The marriages we most admire are the ones where husbands and wives comfortably, fluidly move through each day with the quiet confidence that whatever comes up—whether a menial task or a complex one that requires special expertise—they can count on each other to fill in the gaps. Virtually nothing *can't* be effectively accomplished, because one of them can ably enough handle it and neither of them allows his or her ego to stop them from delegating the task to the best qualified on their team.

In what ways do you find it difficult to bend?

The Vow of Confrontation

Neither love nor intimacy is diminished by compassionate confrontation. Both will be enhanced by your willingness to expose the transgression, determine what led to it, and what can be done to keep it from happening in the future.

"**T**ELL HER, ADAM.**"** He had been urging the man for hours now as they walked along the river. Eve had accused Adam of being lazy and inconsiderate, in front of their friends the night before. She often used social gatherings to "playfully" air her complaints about him, leaving him no way to respond without starting an argument. Adam had carried his anger home with him. "Perhaps I'm being too sensitive," Adam reasoned. "Are you?" The question hung there. They both knew the answer. "Why don't You tell her? She must know." "No," He said in quiet but firm refusal. "I am in no mood for a battle, or for her tears. Besides, it will change nothing." God turned to face The Man with a piercing glare. "But Adam, your worst battles come when you don't speak up, not when you do." As Adam turned to walked away, God reminded him of The Vow of Confrontation.

Though you resist it, I am dead set upon your learning to confront wrongdoing, even when it has been committed by the one you love. Even if confronting it threatens to embarrass you both. Tell the truth anyway. It is the unavoidable starting place on your journey toward reconciliation. Bypass it at your own peril. My efforts to assure you of My love are unceasing, but they are never at the sacrifice of the truth. Though I accept you as you are, I do indeed confront you with the truth, challenging you to become more than you are. You must do as I do.

It can be incredibly difficult to confront your mate when he or she has wronged you. But when necessary, you must do it. Always be willing to listen to each other, but never be afraid to confront each other, and call for change—without apologizing for having done so. Neither love nor intimacy is diminished by firm but compassionate confrontation. On the contrary, both are enriched by your determined efforts to expose the transgression, explore what caused it, and what can be done to repair it and keep it from occurring in the future.

Aladrian and I have struggled over the years with confronting, each in our own way. I, always wanting to move ahead to the next thing on my schedule, find unappetizing the prospect of revisiting an offense from the past. Even if the offense was mere seconds ago, I resent having to stop and invest the time and effort it takes to file my complaint. It feels too much like going backward in time.

Typically, knowing that it must be done, I do a rushed, bare-bones job of it. I dump the hard, cold facts with the crisp brevity of an impatient prosecutor: *"You moved the book I was reading without telling me where you put it. When I wanted it I couldn't find it. In the future I wish you wouldn't touch my books."*

I made myself clear and Aladrian apologizes, but she proceeds to confront me about the "fussy, insensitive" tone of my confrontation. I make a mental note not to bother next time.

Aladrian tells me that she is prone to avoid confronting my wrong-doings because it feels too much like an acknowledgment that she was bothered by what I did. She wishes she weren't as affected by the dumb stuff I may say or do. She much prefers having the satisfaction of knowing that my transgressions had little to no injurious effect on her, that she's too tough to be fazed by my shenanigans. To her, calling it to my attention seems too much like an admission of emotional weakness. After a time, resentment of my thoughtlessness builds in her and she knows that, like it or not, she has to have a word with me: *"You know last week when you . . ."* Now I am angry, not so much about being called on the carpet, but that I have to hear about last week's offenses this week. I confront her about the delay in confronting me. She makes a mental note not to bother next time.

Confrontation can be a messy start to an exchange that ends up focused on the two of you making a better future together, which is exactly the goal of this vow.

What makes confrontation so challenging is our natural disdain for conflict and our intense desire for lasting peace. In seeking the gentler silence of secret-keeping, we create the illusion of peaceful accord. But peace that comes only by default—because you dared not raise a sensitive issue—is not peace at all. It is only denial, where there are no offenses to rectify, and no broken promises that need to be acknowledged. No one's commitment can endure and prosper in a climate where the truth is held captive by fear or self-interest.

We run in terror from the possibility of heated emotions, wounded feelings, or shrunken affection between us. It is often fear and apathy, not tolerance or graciousness or contentment that tempts us to shut up and ignore (at least ostensibly) the way our mates and our marriages are today. A craving for short-term peace tempts us to put off pointing out to each other what must be corrected today if we are to improve our circumstances and protect our commitment to each other.

Despite what your fears may tell you, confrontation is not a commentary on how little love exists between you but how much. No one will exert the efforts and endure the burdens of constructive confrontation where there is no bond of love and commitment. The kind of confrontation in which your sincere aim is to communicate to your mate what he did that did not work for you, and give him the opportunity to decide what, if anything, he is willing to do differently next time. It's not just a chance to vent your anger, display your wounds, and chide the offender.

Here, too, let balance be your watchword. Yours is to speak the

truth in love, both truth and love always. It is the unavoidable starting point on your journey toward resolution and reconciliation. We
bypass this starting point at our own peril. Neither love nor truth
must ever be offered apart from each other. On which end do you
typically show a deficit?

Do you major in truth-telling but know nothing of love? If so,
pushy insistence and shaming rebukes are likely to be your forte.
Yours is a naked truth. Absent is the tender sensitivity that is the gar-
ment of unconditional love. Confrontation without tender affection
is only self-righteousness.

On the other hand, search your ways to determine if you only
speak love (or passively maintain your silence) but seldom declare
the painful truth to your mate, the whole truth without cleverly editing the parts that might stir controversy or demand an explanation.
Love that lacks the sometimes strident declaration of truth is only
self-protection in disguise.

**Are you better at confronting or accepting confrontation?
What can you and your mate learn from
each other's strong suit?**

The Vow of Dismissal

Surprising flashes of your grace and tolerance are much more likely to influence change than a steady stream of complaints and rebukes—even legitimate ones.

EVE HAD BEEN DISTRACTED and out of sorts all evening. Adam had noticed but quickly decided he was far too tired to say or do anything about it. Sleep would be welcome tonight after such a demanding day. He fell into bed, exhausted, choosing to forgo kissing her good night, fearing Eve might take it as an opportunity to pour out her feelings to him. Later, when she came to bed and leaned over for a kiss, Eve found Adam fast asleep. There was a time, she mused, when this would have made her angry with Adam for days. She smiled. Their years together had softened them. So many things didn't matter as much now as they once had. As she lay beside her husband, bathed in the shadows of the moonlit night, she remembered what He had taught her about The Vow of Dismissal.

If I vented every transgression of yours against Me, your ears would be so full of what I find wrong with you that there would be room for little else. The fact that I do not indict you for your every lapse and violation does not mean that you had none. There is so much more to offer the one you love than a recitation of her or his every trespass and the sting of your brand of justice.

What if today you choose to have no complaints? What if, from this sunrise to the next, the one you love doesn't have to defend herself against your accusations or rebuke? What if you simply choose to dismiss all charges? It would mean that this time—not every time—she did not have to endure your chiding her for slighting you or using a snappy tone or not validating, appreciating, or fulfilling you. This time you offer no exasperated roll of your eyes, no put-upon groans, and you do not rush to remind him of how he could have done a better job of it. Of course you and every spouse have the right to lodge a legitimate complaint, but what if today you simply choose to waive that right?

Perhaps you fear that withholding your complaint might encourage the wrong to be repeated. After all, isn't it your responsibility to communicate your partner's deficiencies to help him or her grow into more than who he or she is now? Yes, but for that very reason I urge you to choose to overlook the nonessentials (there are likely to be more of them than real essentials). Surprising flashes of grace and tolerance are much more likely to influence meaningful change than a steady stream of complaints, even legitimate ones. Those who receive a regular diet of complaints eventually become desensitized to them, so that the more there are, the less they pay attention to them. They hear little of the substance of your complaint, after noting that once again you are in complaint mode. But where there has been much tolerance and unexpected offers of mercy, your rare protests will resound with crystal clarity and will be given more serious consideration.

Make no mistake: I am not calling for denial of the facts here. But after full consideration of them, I am urging you to dismiss as many as you possibly can. It is an unconditional pardon. Complete exoneration—without wordy indictments, the threat of wrath to come, and without requiring any applause for having done so.

Because such an unrestrained act of mercy is at times what your mate needs even more than another rebuke for having blown it, another lecture on how to get it right from now on. No one learns to soar if she or he is constantly grounded to answer to new charges of wrongdoing.

I am not suggesting that you ignore every trespass. You mustn't always ignore behaviors that are destructive to your marriage. I am, however, suggesting that you consciously and deliberately stem the tendency to communicate *all* that is wrong, in the obsessive pursuit of justice. It is the legalistic bent of our human nature that causes us to take note of our mate's flaws in such vivid detail that we lose sight of the strengths and virtues that outnumber them.

At some point today seize the opportunity to distance yourself, not from your mate, but from the sound of your dissatisfaction. Today choose to overlook the unsightly and train your eye on the overlooked good that is present in your less-than-perfect mate and marriage. Turn a deaf ear to the cries of your disapproval and let your complaints stay on the tip of your tongue. Don't be surprised if you find observing a complaint-free day blesses you as much or even more than your mate.

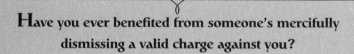

Have you ever benefited from someone's mercifully dismissing a valid charge against you?

The Vow of Clarity

Plainly put expectations and spelled-out agreements make it possible for you to collaborate together as one, though you are, and ever shall remain, two.

THE RAINY SEASON HAD descended harshly upon Eden. The Man and The Woman stayed indoors near the fire. For several months now, they had noticed that their conflicts were taking far less time to resolve. They would confront each other, acknowledge their guilt, and express their apologies within minutes instead of days, as they had in the past. Adam and Eve had become quite proud of themselves. Still, though their disputes were briefer and less contentious, the same issues would inevitably resurface, often within a matter of only a few days. "Nothing is ever finished for good with us," lamented Adam. At exactly the same moment it dawned on them both. Eve spoke first. "Perhaps it is because you apologize sweetly, but seldom say exactly what you will or will not do to keep it from happening again." Adam had another point of view: "No, I suspect it is because you tell me every detail of your complaint, except what you want me to do about it." Then God joined them by the fire. He tutored Adam and Eve on The Vow of Clarity.

Examine closely the nature of My love for you. I have told you with the utmost clarity what I desire and expect of you. And just as precisely I have detailed what you can expect of Me. And, though I know all, I still beckon you to clearly make your requests known to Me. I find pleasure in hearing you risk it all to ask for exactly what you want of Me. A commitment to absolute clarity is what will turn your unvoiced expectations into bold requests and your secret intentions into declared vows.

There are two temptations to which we are all most vulnerable in marriage. One is to use many words, hinting at much, but actually declaring little that anyone could pin us down to, the other is to avoid being specific by saying little (or nothing), then going away assuming you have been completely understood. Both are enticements to avoid clarity because of the risk of raising controversy, upsetting your mate, or getting your own feelings bruised by his or her response. Positive regard for each other, good intentions, and a collaborative nature will never replace spelled-out agreements and plainspoken understanding as the foundation for an indestructible marriage.

No matter how intimate and affectionate your union, you still have two points of view, two separate interests in a dispute, two contrasting (or conflicting) ways of solving problems. Clear communication is what makes it possible for you to collaborate together as one, though you are, and ever shall remain, two.

The necessity of having to speak with crystal clarity can be an uncomfortable reminder that you may be one in spirit yet you're distinctly two in the flesh. Vagueness is the vocabulary of assumption. It is an attempt to avoid making, or calling for, a solid commitment to something precise. Precise commitments subject us to accountability.

One can never be held accountable to what he or she has not clearly stated or directly agreed to. Clarity obligates us to convey the exact nature of our feelings, our intentions, and our desires. Ambiguity allows us to keep them secret, engaging our mates in a futile game of hide-and-seek. Making yourself absolutely clear means no longer being able to take comfort in the excuse that your mate didn't really ignore your request, she or he just misunderstood it. Or that the reason that you have not followed through on the commitment you agreed to was because you are not exactly sure of what your mate is asking of you.

Unspoken assumption cost one couple I was working with every-thing. Throughout their relationship she had frequently *hinted* of her long-held desire to one day marry and raise several children. He, an only child, on many occasions had *hinted* of his long-held desire to marry and have one child upon whom he could lavish all his love. Though at first fully aware of their differing preferences, he assumed that she, having repeatedly heard his hints, had opted to go along with them. After their relationship became serious the topic of chil-dren seldom came up. He and she formed the unspoken assumption that each had become willing to comply with the other's preference. They unwisely assumed that because their mate hadn't raised the issue anymore they were no longer in conflict about it.

The wedding was planned, the dresses, the ring, and the reception hall had all been secured. Then they found out that their differences had not been resolved. They had simply gone underground into the netherworld of unspoken assumptions. They broke it off; bitter feel-ings ensued. Their union had become a casualty of a stunning lack of clarity.

Even at the risk of stating what you believe to be obvious or redun-dant, always clearly verbalize to your mate what you prefer. What you expect; what you intend to do; what you intend not to do. The more significant or sensitive the matter may be, the more important the need for absolute clarity.

At times it may feel to you that your crystal-clear declarations invoke oppressive rules and expectations. You fear it will lead to an insistence upon the law, choking out the spirit of your love. Not so. Clarity does not shackle you by force. It simply binds you to each other with the cords of personal and mutual accountability. These are the handiwork of genuine commitment.

Some spouses hide their true expectations and
commitment behind too many words, others behind
their silence; which kind are you?

The Vow of Retraction

Set the record straight regardless of whether you feel coura-geous or not.

FEAR AND GUILT WEIGHED heavily on Eve. It was as if a giant stone were being pressed against her chest. She knew she had lied to her husband. Much of her afternoon had been spent talking with an acquaintance of Adam's she had run into near the springs. Adam would never approve of her being alone with the man, a shiftless but thoroughly charming fellow who never missed an opportunity to tell Eve how witty and attractive he found her. It had been an innocent enough conversation on what would have been a relatively boring day for Eve. She had convinced herself that it would be best to tell Adam that she had spent the entire afternoon at home tending to chores. The truth would have unnecessarily aroused her husband's suspicion—and his anger. It was more than Eve wanted to contend with; but she was not bearing up very well under the burden of knowing that she had intentionally deceived him. "I must tell Adam I lied," she whispered to herself, trembling at the thought of it. "But how . . . ? And when . . . ? Perhaps it is best that I keep it to myself . . ." From behind her a voice spoke softly but distinctly. "The when and the how are simple, once you understand the why." With that God began to teach her The Vow of Retraction.

One lie is no greater or smaller than another. Certainly there are greater and smaller consequences that result from them, but deceit is not measured by the slightness or the severity of its consequences. There is only the truth; all else is a lie. From the first I always had in mind that marriage is about tearing down walls that separate you, not erecting them. You are wise to heed the dread that you feel after you have deceived your beloved. It is the persistent press of My hand upon your heart and your will, challenging you to go and take back the untruth.

At some point you will know, if you don't already, what it feels like to lie to your mate. First there is the immediate sense of horror and disbelief, as if it could not have been you who did it, but someone you don't know very well at all.

We don't usually invent a 100 percent fabrication. We simply recount the facts with one or two significant details slightly altered or conveniently left out. Or when you are fully aware that your mate has a favorable but inaccurate understanding of something that you did, and rather than correct it, you take the Fifth and enjoy the benefits of your spouse's not knowing the *real* story.

The tendency to alter the truth, even to the tiniest extent, is native to our frail human nature. It is naïve to think that you haven't ever deceived your mate. At best we may assure that we *intend* not to. When we do, we hope that we will prove to be the sort who immediately and humbly admits it.

Act instantly to retract the untruth. Don't contemplate your options, then move after you have reasoned. If you hesitate, fear, guilt, or the passage of time will tempt you to completely redefine your deception to your own self-protective advantage. You'll then characterize it as a "little white lie" or a "necessary evil." Now the lie has begun to lie to you. It has caused you to turn a deaf ear to that still-small voice inside urging you to come clean. At first our untruths only deceive our mates. Then there is a strong, seemingly pure-hearted temptation not to retract, thinking it will help us avoid the hurt feelings (theirs) and embarrassment (ours) that are sure to come with the admission of our guilt. The cliché "What's kept in the dark will always come to light" is frighteningly true.

Once you have allowed time to pass without retracting the lie, you expose yourself, your mate, and your marriage to the eroding effects of it. It is painful enough admitting to having lied; even worse is not to admit the lie and end up caught in it. Then the lie you found so convenient at one time will turn on you to destroy your credibility and is likely to dramatically diminish your mate's willingness to trust you, even in matters that have nothing to do with what you lied about. Your remorse about the harm you've done can be eclipsed by your mate's nagging suspicion that you are not really sorry that you lied, just sorry that you were caught.

A friend of ours with a long, solid marriage made a careless miscalculation on his tax return that eventually resulted in a sizable, unexpected bill for penalties and interest. Embarrassed, he kept the news from his wife, borrowed the money to pay the debt, and when the subject of household finances came up he led his wife to believe that "nothing new" had happened. Months later, after the taxes and the loan had been paid off, his wife discovered documents about them. She was mortified, not about the money but that her husband had "twisted the truth" and never chose to let her in on the deception. It was a very long time ago, but the years of accumulated trust she had in her husband have still not totally been restored.

It is naïve to declare that you will never deceive your mate. You only mean you hope not to do so intentionally, regularly or maliciously. But if and when you do, decide now that continuing in the lie is not an option. Lies separate the two of you from living the same reality at the same time. It is the very opposite of intimacy when one of you knows the whole truth and one of you only thinks you do.

Pointing out your deception will expose your selfishness but it will also affirm your trustworthiness, which is the very foundation of love and commitment.

When the truth is difficult to tell, pray for the courage, then open your mouth and set the record straight regardless of whether you feel courageous or not.

What's the most intimidating aspect of having to expose
your own deceit? What makes it so?

The Vow of Synchronization

Make the outrageous commitment to travel outside your own time zone. Pursue collaboration, though the process may be annoyingly faster or slower than you'd like.

VE KNEW BOTH TRAILS well. One was rocky and steep, but it would get them to the top quicker. The other would take longer to travel, but it would lead them to the most glorious views along its ascent. "We'll take the short trail," Adam decided for them. "But Adam, we're not trying to rush to the top of the hill, we are trying to enjoy the journey as well. How we get there is just as important . . ." "Fine, then let's follow the scenic trail," Adam interrupted. "Wait, Adam. I'm trying to remember how long it takes to go that way. It would be a pity to go the longer way and not arrive in time to see the sun set." "Oh, Eve, please pick one of them. Must we waste the entire day deciding?" Adam urged. Eve could sense her husband's growing impatience, but she felt she needed a few more moments to consider the wisest choice. Then The Creator appeared just ahead where the trail forked. As He walked toward The Man and The Woman, He began to speak to them concerning The Vow of Synchronization.

I firmly believe in the possibility of the two of you becoming one. It was My idea in the first place. Though your personal timing vastly differs from each other, you have the ability to be synchronized if you are willing to do as I do. Will you submit yourselves to the ticking of your mate's clock? It is bound to be noticeably slower or faster than your own. It is exactly what I do for you. Your response to My desires and My instructions is often maddeningly slow. I wait. At times you make choices in haste and expect Me to catch up to you and snatch you from the unexpected consequences of your impulsive decisions. And I am there. Though My timing is not like yours, I never leave you to go it alone. Will you do with each other what I do with you?

If you haven't already, you will soon discover that you and your partner are seldom perfectly synchronized. One of you is certain to be more of a "plotter and planner." You approach making decisions and taking action with a slow, contemplative hesitancy. To you, "going with your gut feelings" seems careless and impulsive. Any decisive action occurs only "in due time," after you have carefully mulled over every available option.

Since it is true that opposites *are* attracted to each other, plotters and planners are typically married to those who aren't. They have spouses who are almost certain to be "movers and shakers," who favor a much quicker approach—the direct, nonstop transitions from question to answer and from decision made to decision acted upon.

The more significant the decision, the more vital the need to take action, the more clearly it can be seen which of you is which. Plotters and planners will feel rushed, sensing you are being forcibly moved toward conclusions and commitments you are not yet ready to make. Your reflex response is to slow down even more and proceed with even greater caution. Or, when you feel especially rushed by an impatient mate, you are likely to become overwhelmed and avoid any decision or action at all.

A mover and shaker, on the other hand, feels compelled to advance with yet swifter dispatch so as to keep from becoming bogged down in her mate's lethargy. She fears that further delay will result only in more wheel spinning and the time-consuming analysis that brings progress to a grinding halt. An issue left unresolved, a course of action left undecided, is hell on earth to a mover and shaker.

When it comes to major decision making I am a classic plotter and planner. I mull every available option to weigh the predicted risks versus the rewards, earnestly attempting to identify the decision that is least likely to subject me to future regret. Whether it's a choice between eyeglasses or contact lenses, the fish or the chicken, paying by check or with cash, mulling takes time. A marriage can be blessed by a plotter and planner's exceptional analytical prowess—and cursed by his reluctance to go ahead and "pull the trigger."

Aladrian is definitely not a plotter and planner. The quintessential mover and shaker, she dreads the possibility of being buried alive in a mountain of options. She is naturally inclined to go with the option that is most readily accessible and somehow "just feels right." Movers and shakers steer clear of complications and earnestly seek to get to the finish line. Marriages can be blessed by movers and shakers' keen intuition—and cursed by their haste.

To Aladrian my mulling is like taking a cruise through a sea of molasses. Her way of getting to the finish line feels like a thoughtless coin toss to me.

Collaborating to make decisions together was brutal, if not impossible. Neither of us had the slightest bit of appreciation for each other's style and frequently told each other so. For years our individual paces were so out of sync that we ended up dividing major decisions between us, like pieces of personal property. *This one's yours. That one's mine.* We each assumed sole proprietorship of various key decisions that affected both of us. Though it kept us from the stress of enduring each other's "unreasonable" pace, it made impossible the kind of collaboration necessary to an develop intimate partnership.

For us the catalyst for change was the house-hunting process. After being shown over a dozen homes, I, of course, wanted some more time to analyze our options and to make the perfect choice. Aladrian wanted us to go with the second house we had seen. It was the one that (according to her recollection) had made us both smile upon entering it—and the one that was ready for immediate move-in. I felt rushed. She felt paralyzed.

Our mutual frustration led us to the "accidental" discovery of a practical way to synchronize our clocks. Instead of letting me retreat to my extended mulling, Aladrian gave me a one-week deadline. I could feel free to mull and ponder, but at the end of the seven days I had to emerge with my top choice. Having a deadline helped me to focus and to avoid the interminable analysis that led to wasted time and already-sold houses.

In turn I challenged her to put off making a final choice for seven days, after which she would have to let me know not only her choice but five concrete reasons why *that* house as opposed to one of the others. Having to think and wait forced Aladrian to stop and consider what features really mattered most to her for our new home and to weigh previously unidentified pros and cons about each house. After a little mulling she picked a different house.

The collaborative process of decision making and action taking cannot happen without the slower pace of careful deliberation synchronized with the brisker pace of bold decisiveness. Rather than resisting the pace by which your spouse makes decisions and takes action, make adjustments to your own by allowing your collaboration to be sometimes a little (and sometimes a lot) slower or faster than you'd prefer. Choose to tolerate being slightly outside your own time zone. It is in synchronizing the two that you can rise above the liabilities of your personal paces and benefit together from the assets found in each other's.

Have you invested as much time considering the possible benefits of your mate's personal timing as you have complaining about the drawbacks of it?

The Vow of Vulnerability

Keeping ourselves to ourselves is an attempt to safely hide. Only when you commit to expose yourself anyway do you ensure the possibility of your feelings being accurately taken into account by your mate.

EVE WAS CERTAIN there was something troubling Adam. She was equally certain that it had something to do with her; something that would not go away on its own. Her husband's mood had been shifting all morning. At times Adam was sullen and detached. At other times harsh and ill-tempered. Through it all he refused to offer any clues as to what might be bothering him. Finally he left abruptly, without a good-bye. Eve resented that her husband's comings and goings held such sway over her emotions. Peering into the reflection pond, she practiced her most unaffected and indifferent expressions. She would make sure that upon his return, Adam would not have the pleasure of seeing how much his mysterious brooding troubled her. He had returned at nightfall. "I am much better now, Eve, but I'd rather not talk about this morning. Let's just go on from here, all right?" he said quietly, then turned without awaiting a response from her. "That's just fine with me, Adam, as I have neither the time nor the interest to be concerned with it anyway," Eve said, dismissing him as she pretended to busy herself with her braids. Adam was taken aback. "What is the matter, Eve?" The Woman answered as she rose to leave the room. "Nothing. Nothing at all." Her departure was blocked by God's sudden appearance in the doorway. Upon entering He immediately began to teach them The Vow of Vulnerability.

You say that you want the kind of marriage in which you are deeply known and understood by your beloved. You say that you do not want fortresses of secrecy that exile you from each other. Yet when I look into your heart I see pockets of darkness, the telltale signs of well-secured hiding places. I created marriage to be the most intimate of human relationships. Hiding of any kind for any reason will never serve you well.

It is not difficult to understand the appeal of our hiding places. We all have had them since the first time we let someone we loved see our true, unmasked selves and the person abruptly lost interest and fled. If love can be so dangerous, we reasoned, then we must be ready to retreat swiftly to a safe haven where our feelings are not so easily known, thus making us less vulnerable to the threat of attack or abandonment.

We hide our shortcomings to avoid ridicule. We hide our desires and expectations to keep from being denied them. We hide our fragile insecurities to keep anyone from cruelly having his or her way with them. Hiding out is our way of defending against emotional devastation.

In marriage, however, our greatest losses occur when we continue to run away from each other to the safety of our personal havens of refuge. The silent, fearful refusal to share your thoughts and feelings, your highest hopes as well as your deepest fears and your troubling questions, leaves little room for your mate to know you well enough to love you in the best way possible.

Over time secret hiding places become violent battlefields. When we keep choosing silent retreat over the certain vulnerabilities of painful disclosure we provoke each other's detachment or wrath, which have otherwise been avoided by letting your mate in close enough to profoundly know you.

Only that which you are willing to expose has any chance of getting a positive response from your mate or, at the very least, understood and taken into account by her. Concealment is fed by fear and the singular pursuit of one's own sense of safety. If you allow the hidden places in you to stay hidden, you send a clear message that the spiritual intimacy of your marriage is of secondary importance, while protecting yourself from the threat of rejection is primary.

When your mate is slow to disclose himself to you do not take it as a personal affront. His defensive strategy is less about shutting you out than it is about shutting himself in from the intimidating prospect of earning your disapproval. A hiding place can be dismantled only by the one who erected it. Your invasive probing and guilt-inducing pleas for disclosure only result in more defensiveness, not less.

Patience and the bold refusal to indulge yourself is the only way to reduce the amount of hiding that takes place in your marriage. Though it may not be easy it can be done, if you are first willing to confront your tendency to hide. When something repeatedly touches a nerve, exposes a wound, or threatens a sensitivity in you, practice speaking up about it to your mate. Open your mouth and share your concerns. Acknowledge to your mate and to yourself that what you share are not permanent, fully formed declarations of reality but a report on the current (and perhaps still-evolving) state of your thoughts and feelings. Your courage to expose your favorite hiding places is the best means of encouraging your mate to share his.

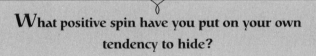

What positive spin have you put on your own tendency to hide?

The Vow of Deprioritizing

There is no need to do it *all* right, or to do it all right now. If you focus only on the challenging demands of married life, your relationship will be all earnestness and hard effort with little of the spontaneity and joyful abandon necessary for the long haul.

THE SUN HAD JUST RISEN when The Man and The Woman met The Creator in the meadows not far from their home. Married only a short time, the two had already concluded that having an excellent marriage would require their constant vigilance over every detail. They spent a good portion of each day assessing their progress, dissecting each conversation, questioning every mood and the nuances of every word or facial expression. This morning, as at every sunrise, they would carefully pour out their petitions to God hoping He'd offer any special revelations that would keep their marriage from ever falling apart. The Man and The Woman believed that they could not be too cautious when there was something this important at stake. It was not until mid-morning that they finally ended their anxious pleadings. "Now, God, tell us what we must do to tend ably to these grave matters we have brought before You," Adam beseeched Him. "Yes, only show us and we will do it, even if it takes all our strength to do so," added Eve. When He spoke it was not what they had expected. "Go back to your bed until noonday; then wander at your leisure throughout the entire Garden. Jest with each, speaking only of foolish things. Things that are so meaningless and ridiculous that you cannot help but laugh aloud." Then God left them to begin learning what He would later reveal to be The Vow of Deprioritizing.

Despite your declarations that you know I have everything under My control, you have been known to cower, fearful that your marriage could come apart at the seams at any moment. Your terror, though discreetly hidden from view, comes from the misbelief that you are The Guardian of your marriage. If you will relax your fearful grip upon it, you will suddenly discover unpredicted opportunities for genuine enjoyment of each other.

Most of us wholeheartedly embrace the ominous notion that marriage is serious business. The very mention of the word *marriage* conjures up images of two earnest lovers attempting a dangerously unsure climb up Mount Everest. Being bound to each other, they fear that one false move, one tiny misstep by either, would plummet them both to a rocky grave. When you view your marriage only as a matter of life and death, you maintain a white-knuckle grip on every trivial detail and choke the joy right out of it. None of us can afford for our marriages to be all serious business.

I once stopped to watch the lunch-hour ice-skaters at a large rink inside a shopping mall. Every face told a story. Most of them, whether masters or novices, were clearly having an incredibly good time as they glided around the rink.

Their fun was not without some risk, however. Some would take a slide, then quickly regroup, taking it all in stride. Others would completely fall down upon the ice, laugh out loud, and get up for another spin. They didn't let a slip, a slide, or a full tumble to the ground keep them from having a great time.

There was a lone skater with a look of sheer terror on his face. He was so intent upon not taking a fall, not bumping against another skater, and definitely not (heaven forbid) looking foolish that he confined himself to a tiny corner of the rink, barely moving more than a couple of feet before stopping, as if to marvel at his minute progress. This tensely vigilant skater never once splattered onto the ice, but he didn't appear to be having very much fun either.

When you are focused only on the challenging demands required to keep a marriage from going under, you will always be stiffly at attention, excessively sensitive to even the slightest shifts of your or your mate's moods, or the ever changing circumstances in which you find yourselves. Your life together will be all earnestness and hard work, but will possess little of the spontaneity and joyful abandon we all hope our marriages would include.

I once counseled a couple who, after working successfully to resolve the issue that brought them into therapy, insisted on continuing their weekly appointments with me. Rather than go home to celebrate their new and improved marriage, they wanted to stick around, nervously anticipating that some other problem would surely surface that would also need to be fixed. "Our marriage is too important to play around with," the husband gravely informed me.

Theirs was the marital perfectionist's classic fear: that if any one of their "issues" ever was downgraded from life or death urgency, everything would come crashing down around them. Thus, all matters between them were subjected to endless analysis and discussion. Virtually nothing was viewed as nonthreatening or insignificant. Everything had to be "dealt with"—every altogether meaningless word, or change of inflection, every ambiguous expression, every questionable gesture, decision or response—all were placed squarely under the microscope for a thorough examination.

We vow to let nothing get past us. Though for a time it feels mature and responsible to be so vigilant, it inevitably makes shared laughter and the possibility of relaxing and exposing our unguarded, authentic selves around each other nearly impossible.

Consider deprioritizing your own obsession with trivialities. Light-heartedness and the relaxed pleasure of each other's company can benefit you more than the exhausting attention paid to every relational loose end and your wasted time and energy to get them all straightened out. For many couples married life would be far less tense and much more enjoyable if for example, they'd:

- **Pursue superficiality.** Observe at least one day a week when "working on our marriage" (conflict, financial and administrative concerns, and other energy-sapping relational issues) is strictly off-limits. On that day give yourselves over to mindless conversations, teasing, flirting, and the enjoyment of the pleasures of each other's company.

- **Give up.** Where possible hire someone else to take over for one of the areas of responsibility that trigger so much anxiety and effort (housekeeping, bill paying, cooking, "counseling" each other).
- **Schedule a reunion.** Renew close contact with other couples who make you *laugh*, not just the ones who make you *think*.
- **Look beyond "Us."** Find some needs and problems outside your marriage to crusade on behalf of, instead of keeping such tunnel-vision focus on your marital woes.

Every matter is not worthy of resolution. Some must be allowed to simply pass, unexamined, without either of you having complete understanding as to what, if anything, they may have meant. Those issues, like shooting stars, will appear, burn brightly, and pass quickly on their own, never to be seen again. Shooting stars need only be seen, not studied. Meaningful issues between you that really do demand your attention have a strange way of resurfacing over and over, each time more insistently. Adopt a policy of letting them merit your attention only after a return appearance or two.

Making your marriage a haven of peace and good humor where two lovers are becoming genuine friends is available to those who are willing to let their list of priorities be a very short one.

You have stood stiffly at attention, guarding the palace gates long enough. Now enter into the joys and pleasures behind them. Relax—all is not as important as it may seem.

In what ways do you and your mate take yourselves
far too seriously?

The Vow of Authority

The bold commitment to challenge your mate to act in consideration of your best interest and not just his or her own.

VE SAT STRAIGHT UP in bed, suddenly wide awake but still completely exhausted. It was well past midnight when the noisy clamoring began, then the repeated, full-throated call of her name had snatched her from a deep sleep. It was Adam returning from several days of hunting in the eastern forests. He would now expect her to get up to view the hunt's yield, and to hear his long, breathless account of every chase and each kill. He could go on until daybreak, fully expecting Eve's properly enthusiastic and undivided attention until then. Adam seemed to come alive during the late night hours. Eve preferred retiring early and was at her most alert in the morning after a sound night's rest. They discussed, rather argued, about this each time he returned from a hunt in the middle of the night. "If you truly loved me," he'd say, "you wouldn't find it bothersome to sit up with me, no matter how tired you are." "And if you really cared about me, you'd let this keep until morning when I am well rested. This just isn't right, Adam," she'd counter. But, as usual, feeling trapped and guilty, she gave in. Eve rose to sit with her husband. "God, make me better at letting him have his way," she silently prayed. In an instant The Creator appeared before her casting a questioning look. "But Eve, what makes you think you must always let him get his way?" She suddenly remembered what He had taught her and instantly moved to act on it. Eve spoke with sincere affection, but in a firm, measured tone that left no room for dispute. "Welcome home, my darling. I am anxious to hear every detail—but in the morning, *not tonight*." With that she turned and headed back to their bedchamber. As The Man sat too stunned to protest, God joined him and reminded him of The Vow of Authority.

To everything there is a season. There will be times in marriage when you will have to draw the line. You must refuse to cooperate with an

unjust or unrealistic expectation or demand when put upon you by the
one you love. There are some requests made of you to which the answer
must be no. Dare not pretend that it is always yours to satisfy your mate's
every whim and desire with no regard as to whether you find it fair or
that I find it righteous.

A favorite book in my library bears the title *Love Must Be Tough*. The
idea that love (especially the kind required for a solid marriage)
rightly includes taking an at-times firm, immovable stance can be off-
putting to those who think only of the commitment's gentle, ever
accommodating aspects. To many it seems impossible to both boldly
exercise one's personal authority and express one's unconditional love
at the same time. As if you'd have to momentarily stop doing the one
to be able to do the other. Can you really love someone if you just
responded to an expectation that person has of you by saying (and
meaning) "No, I won't. I refuse . . . ?"

> *"No, I refuse to lie for you or for anyone."*
> *"No, I refuse to join you in wasting what God has given us on some-*
> *thing that is destructive to us."*
> *"No, I refuse to sit idly by and help you to mistreat me or yourself."*
> *"No, I refuse to ignore, deny, or distort reality in order to keep from*
> *displeasing you."*

Exercising your authority has nothing to do with giving orders,
demanding that your spouse bow in submission to your whims. Alas,
not even in your own home have you been crowned Ruler of the
World. What it does mean is boldly challenging your mate to consider and act in accordance with your best interests and not just her
own. It's standing up to an injustice to say, *"That doesn't work for me.*

I can't join in you in that," even at the risk of your beloved's displeasure—and your own uneasy feelings.

What you say no to reveals to your mate the bedrock principles that you hold to be moral and just, thus nonnegotiable. Some marriage partners fall into the trap of believing that sincere love requires that you simply give, do, become what is expected of you. As if genuine commitment answers only in the affirmative. Marriage is no place for yes-men and yes-women. For a time we feel flattered by their signing off on our every idea and expectation. We like it when they follow our lead and get behind our agenda. Soon, however, we begin to suspect that virtually anything we propose they will endorse simply because we proposed it, not because they personally agree with its merits. We know little to nothing about where they themselves stand on the issue.

People who never exercise their personal right of refusal are hiding themselves behind a mirror that clearly reflects their mate's preferences and expectations, but keeps their own from being seen and known at all. The hidden forfeit the opportunity to be truly known and to have their values understood and respected. Another reason it's so important to come out from behind it and authoritatively take a moral position is that you can powerfully influence each other's level of moral judgment and integrity when you do. We tend to rise to new levels of righteousness and maturity when we are influenced by the example of someone we love.

A former client, Jim, desperately wanted to marry Michelle, his dream woman. She was happily in agreement, if, and only if, Jim would "give back" the foster son he was in the process of adopting. It was an uneasy dilemma for Jim. The boy was his heart, and Jim had absolutely no intention of going back on his commitment to father him. Still, he didn't want to lose Michelle.

Instead of exercising his personal "right to refuse" authority to say to her, "No, I can't give you what you are asking. It would be wrong," he said nothing (and did nothing) about the issue, hoping that his bride-to-be would eventually change her mind without his having to speak his. Michelle interpreted his silence (and his presentation of a three-carat engagement ring) as Jim's agreement to her terms. Only many weeks later, after Michelle had spent several thousand dollars on a wedding gown, did Jim speak out. Even then it was not to authoritatively voice his true convictions, but to criticize Michelle for not withdrawing her prerequisite to accommodate his nonnegotiable commitment. Thankfully Jim and Michelle chose not to marry each other. They discovered, the hard way, that love doesn't mean forfeiting one's personal authority. Hard lessons are often the best-learned ones. Those who won't exercise their authority make their mates responsible for figuring out their inner convictions without their having to state them and uphold them.

Even those of us who relish the spotlight dread the possibility that our mates will label us self-righteous and stubborn if we declare and firmly stick to our personal moral convictions. We'd prefer not to be seen as boat rockers or crusaders for our just cause. Because they have taken an unpopular position, crusaders are conspicuous and thus naturally vulnerable to their mate's protest and even ridicule. Even though I respect the differences between us, it's so much easier and comfortable when Aladrian and I have perfect consensus on a matter. Refusals are controversial. Though I am opposed to it in principle, in actual practice my nature is slanted toward avoiding controversy in our marriage whenever possible.

You have the authority (and with practice you will develop the ability) to speak your mind even when it is controversial. Even when it makes you sound stubborn and hard-nosed. Be willing to live with the consequences of assuming your rightful authority, your self-respect, as well as your mate's ability to know the values and convictions that you believe are at stake. To speak and act graciously, but assertively and unapologetically, is to display love and truth suited in the gleaming armor of strength.

How willing are you to rock the boat?

The Vow of Acceptance

We choose each other because of the appealing differences between our mates and ourselves. Then, of necessity, we must make the outrageous commitment to accept the manifestations of those differences as seen in what they nearly never initiate and what you virtually always have to initiate.

S HE WATCHED ADAM AS HE stepped out of the tide pool. He shook his head wildly to get the excess water out of it. This was when The Woman found her husband most attractive. She wished it were not so. They had not made love in weeks. "And it will probably not be for a long time to come," she muttered to herself as she turned away from his seductive form. Eve had grown tired of feeling as if she had to initiate everything. If there were strained feelings between them, she would be the first to bring it up. If the children needed to be disciplined it would only happen after Eve raised the issue. Arguing, making up, trying something new, remembering special occasions—all seemed to require her leading. Constantly having to ask, remind, or start it first in order to spur Adam's involvement had brought her to the point of frustration. Eve had now determined that if they were to ever resume having sexual relations Adam would have to initiate them. Without meaning to, she turned and caught sight of him reclining under the date palm. Tiny beads of water glistened in the sun, then rolled off Adam's muscled torso. "Why doesn't he ever bother to cover himself?" she groused. There beside the tide pool, with Adam's sculpted form filling her gaze, God spoke to Eve concerning The Vow of Acceptance.

I have watched your singular efforts when you have had to be The One Who Must. . . . I hear the frustrated, unspoken questions within: "Why must it always be me?" I have had to be The One Who Must . . . in My relationship with you. It is always I who have taken the first step to establish it and to sustain it. I know it does not always seem fair, especially according to your limited assessment. A balanced distribution of the burdens of initiating action must be measured by examining all the countless areas of responsibility—not merely the one or two that are

*your own personal priorities. Should you consider each and every one,
you will likely see what I see. That both of you in different ways, at different times, have been The One Who Must. . . . Take care that you do
not overlook the areas in which it has been your mate because you are so
fixed on protesting the areas in which it is now you.*

In marriage you will seldom get a strict fifty-fifty division of anything.
There is virtually nothing that each of you will do anywhere near as
much as the other. So much of your life together as husband and wife
involves responsibilities you must take on. Communicating, expressing affection, setting policies, making strategies, problem-solving
obstacles, resolving conflicts, managing your finances, your children,
and your future—all are necessary obligations that matter to you
both but are unlikely to be shared in equally. The simple truth is, in
some of these areas you will typically play the leading role and in others (usually ones you value less) your mate will. The problem is we
are at least a little less likely to notice that they are leading in *something* because we are so busy noticing the things in which we always
have to take the lead.

Acceptance is a practical vow that may run alarmingly counter to
your natural, logical expectations. In almost every individual area of
married life, you may notice that you or your mate has emerged as
"The One." The One who nearly always initiates, oversees, or
assumes the bulk of responsibility for maintaining that area of your
marriage or your home.

Early in our marriage I took Aladrian to task because I was nearly
always The One who had to see that things like broken doorknobs or
cracked windowpanes were repaired. I resented the fact that if I
silently waited for her to handle it sometimes, we'd go on indefinitely
using a screwdriver as a makeshift doorknob and masking tape to seal

a crack in the windowpane. I wondered why she couldn't see to those needs at least some of the time.

I nursed my outrage at the injustice until Aladrian pointed out what I had never considered: that as much as I appreciated the fun of having houseguests (it was often my idea), she was always The One who did the inviting and the special preparations for their coming. If she did not do it I would only *wish* for weekend guests but never make a move to ensure we had them.

Though I alone saw to repairs, I could never again truthfully say it was unjust for me to have to. It became clear that it was simply the part I played in meeting a unique practical need that was important to both of us. Neither of us had exploited the other.

We had demanded justice and equity be manifest in our own tiny, limited area of concern. By looking beyond it to the many other areas of responsibility that we would normally take for granted, we realized that overall distribution of the functions was fairly balanced.

At times it may appear that were you to suddenly stop your initiating in that area, then it would never be a part of your marriage again. I suspect your prediction is likely to be accurate. How willing have you been to accept this fact without repeated volcanic tirades against the injustice or settling into seething resentment? Or have you altogether refused to continue initiating in that area rather than endure the burdensome responsibilities of being cast as The One who always has to make this particular thing happen—if it's going to happen at all?

The One Who Must initiate lovemaking, or who must bring up a thorny issue. The One Who Must press for a corporate decision to be made or Who Must lead in disciplining the children or settling the dispute of figuring out what is to be spent, saved, or given.

In a few instances the answer is as obvious as the ring on your finger. You are The One because you simply will not clearly and consistently voice your complaint and make specific, kindly requests that your mate could initiate more often too. We often have a great disdain for loving gestures that must be verbalized to our mate rather than foreknown by them.

In some matters, you are The One who initiates simply because you are The One who holds such high standards and expectations in that area. Whether you admit it or not, you are the responsible party because you are the only one to whom that particular issue matters. Thus you must pay a higher cost—the burden of being The One. In any given area the weightier responsibilities of initiating naturally fall to The One whose standards are highest.

Usually, though, it is neither the propensity to make requests, nor your exceedingly high standards, that consistently cast you or your mate as The One in a given area of responsibility. More often than not, it is simply because you both possess distinctly different and highly complex personalities, interests, abilities, and experiences that make you feel more attracted to and competent in a particular task. You married each other because of your attraction to your mate in all his or her gloriously appealing differences from you. Now you must be willing to accept these differences manifest by what you almost always initiate, and what you never initiate. In marriage you will seldom, if ever, achieve a fifty-fifty division in any one area. Expect to see justice and equality only when considering the whole endless list of roles and functions needed to keep your marriage and your home afloat. You are The One who does the laundry when you've both run out of shirts. Your mate's The One who brings the humor when your home is short on laughter. You are The One who has to tend to the paperwork. Your mate is The One who first models forgiving and moving on. You are The One who makes all the dentist appointments. Your mate is The One who always has to remind you both to pray.

From this day forward until death parts you, will you make the extraordinary commitment to accept a contented, unlimited tolerance of the unique life the two of you have to share? Will you accept that you are—and perhaps forever shall be—The One Who Must . . . in certain vital areas, and that your mate is The One Who Must . . . in others?

In what marital responsibilities are you virtually always The One? What has it cost you and your marriage for you to persist in considering it "completely unacceptable" rather than simply undesirable?

The Vow of Patience

You will desperately desire necessary changes in your mate, your marriage, or yourself. Though you may work diligently to make them happen, you will have to wait, only knowing *what* you want but having no clue *when* it will appear.

FOR SEVERAL NIGHTS THEY had kept their distance from each other, praying silently—and separately—before retiring. After years of suffering what Eve viewed as Adam's defensiveness and impenetrable arrogance, his apologies and promises to change mattered little. Likewise Adam had come to believe that if Eve was ever going to stop being so quick-tempered and confrontational, it would have happened by now. "It has only gotten worse with time," he observed to himself. Neither of them could imagine that there was anything possible that would make any difference at this point. Both had said as much when they had brought their complaints to God. He would always listen intently, then offer the same curious response: *"Wait until tomorrow."* Each night for six nights, *". . . Tomorrow."* By the seventh night neither The Man nor The Woman felt like talking to God about it again. They did not want to embrace, or lie close to each other. They definitely did not want to dare expect anything of their future together. That night God visited Adam and Eve and finally detailed to them The Vow of Patience.

My ways are not your ways. You are only focused on building a better "now," I on building a better "forever." I have built both the slow and the swift into My creation. I alone reserve the right to determine into which category your awaited desire falls. Have I not been willing to wait for you daily, hoping you will choose to spend even a few moments in communion with Me? Sometimes the wait is long and fruitless, but never is it in vain. I know well of waiting and I am still waiting for you to rise and act upon the thing that is right to do once I have revealed it to you. Yet because of your fear or fatigue, or the childish notion that you know the better way, you hesitate. I wait in patience and unbridled anticipa-

tion for what is yet to be. I wait because you are worth the wait. Will you do as I do?

Being married challenges you to new, sometimes excruciating levels of patience often with no sign that the good upon which you wait is coming soon. You'll want to give to each other, and get from each other, the most seasoned, unconditional devotion as quickly as possible. Though it is a worthy desire, it is not instantly achieved. You will have to endure a wait for its manifestation. You will wait, sometimes with the most fragile faith, only knowing what you want, but having no idea when it will appear.

We often resist waiting (and move impulsively to make our demands, express our displeasure, or sever our ties) due to a mistaken belief that waiting patiently is equivalent to doing nothing at all about our circumstances. Our patience begins to smell suspiciously like the idle state of passivity for which, we suspect, we'll get nothing in the end. To us passivity equals powerlessness. We consider the acknowledgment of powerlessness absolutely unacceptable.

A long-married friend of mine told me that he avoids frustrations and disappointment in his marriage by having no expectations for anything to ever get better. That way, he proudly explained, "I'll be pleasantly surprised if things do improve." His wife complains that my friend never takes note of any progress in any area of their marriage. He prides himself on his sober pragmatism when he predicts, "If she hasn't bothered to watch her weight after all this time, then she's going to be overweight the rest of her life." My friend is thoroughly convinced that after a few years have passed, spouses and marriages can't improve very much. So when some positive changes do occur he never acknowledges it because it would blow his theory to bits.

When frustrated we often go so far as to demand immediate delivery of what we believe is clearly, justly due us—an explanation, an apology, an answer, a show of affection or concern—and, at times, it will be slow in coming. Impatient spouses won't be able to endure the delay, hopeful ones feed on their hope until the day of delivery.

A client of mine once told me of her hope that her husband would ease up on his romance with the television and choose to spend more time enjoying her company. Eventually, weary with frustration and disappointment, she told herself that she no longer even cared. I challenged her to admit that she really wasn't being truthful to herself. When she reclaimed her nearly lost hope she determined that rather than constantly berating her husband for his love affair with television (thus repeatedly indicating to him what she *didn't* want from him), she'd make sure to express her delight and appreciation for those rare times when he *did* make himself available to spend time with her. She did away with her demands and threats but not her anticipation that change would come. The wait was difficult, but it had become more bearable. Her husband soon noticed the appealing change in her mood and her attitude toward him. Eventually the idea of spending more time enjoying his wife instead of TV reruns became desirable enough for him to hit the off button on his remote control.

We all suffer with our bouts of impatience with our mates, our circumstances, and ourselves. Waiting can be so monotonous and unsettling. When you are offered the choice of having what you yearn for right now or much later, the choice is obvious. The temptation is to abandon our hopes after they become weakened by age. We have a compulsion to reduce a lofty but delayed hope to a readily available but inferior alternative. Left to your own devices you can certainly create a temporary, man-made version of what you desire from your mate. And though you may temporarily distract yourself from the discomfort of waiting, ultimately you will have done yourself little good.

A lasting, flourishing marriage grows that way over the span of many seasons in the same way that we must wait for the return of spring flowers, or winter's snow, or for midnight to give way to day-break. We wait without knowing the exact moment our wait will end, the moment the change or resolution will finally occur. God tends not to let us have a peek into His appointment book. We wait know-ing that we do not have sovereign control over any element of our marriage, including its waiting periods. To endure the wait, with all its mysteries, is to put your trust in God's ability to decide the slow and the swift; and to decide what will, in the end, benefit you most.

Those who can maintain the embrace of long-held hopes are the ones for whom change does indeed occur. They are the ones who can appreciate and celebrate that there is always more to come if you will look for it. Those who don't expect change will never notice when it occurs. It wasn't wisdom that clued them in; it was pessimism that blinded them. Dust off your long-abandoned hopes for your mar-riage. Proudly consider them valid desires, not "must-have" goals. To whatever extent you are able, act in ways that contribute to their being realized in your marriage.

Forever is divided into three parts: what was, what is and what shall be. Make peace with the fact that much of what you want for your marriage must be held in hope—unannounced by what has been, unconfirmed by what is, until the appearance of what shall be. At times getting to what shall be—change, fulfillment, resolution—will mean having to endure an extended wait.

What's the important lesson you need to learn from the example set by the most patient person you know?

The Vow of Reaching Out

Everything you need to develop and maintain an indestructible marriage is available, but it is not always found inside you, but around you, from others who know something that you don't.

HEY SAT IN STONY SILENCE watching a brook chase itself toward the Euphrates. All the words had already been spoken between them. They had no brilliant ideas, no energy left to act upon them. Every tear had been shed. Reason and emotion had each had its turn, leaving The Man and The Woman feeling inept, feeling like failures. Just then, a flash of something in the water caught their attention. A perfect green leaf hurried along the current like a small, unmanned vessel submitting to its circumstances, helpless and hopeless. One pair of empty eyes met the other just long enough for wordless agreement to flit between them. They were sitting in silence when God appeared. "You're so quiet," He said. "Is everything all right?" They smiled uncomfortably. Adam took Eve's hand. "Everything's fine. We're just fine." Eve woodenly nodded her assent. The Creator's response was swift. "You are not fine! You're drowning! Whom do you think you are fooling?" As they sat stunned and convicted, God taught Adam and Eve The Vow of Reaching Out.

It is neither an accident nor a miscalculation when I allow your mar-riage to suffer what you consider the insufferable. It is I adjusting the gross weight of your needs until they are far heavier than either of you can bear alone. I am working to increase your ability to bear up under life's heartiest challenges and to survive them triumphantly. When your trial is burdensome enough, mysterious enough, long enough, you will be confronted with the absolute insufficiency of your natural abilities and the utter fruitlessness of your attempts to navigate yourselves out of your troubles. You will need Me. That is not new. You always need Me. But it is when you are in over your heads, when what you need is beyond your reach, that you will believe you need Me. Then I will put you in

close proximity to a gift of wisdom that you and your marriage are greatly in need of. Pay close attention; you will learn something that you did not know but have sorely needed to. Will you readily accept My assistance, if you must receive it from those I have placed there to help you when you cannot help yourself?

Will you reach out for what you do not have yourselves, if it must come from someone else who possesses the wisdom and experience your marriage sorely needs? Mere mortals are the divinely appointed agents of the miraculous. It works beautifully, unless you suffer from the notion that you ought to be able to handle everything yourselves. Those who believe that seldom admit that they do, but live completely faithful to their unspoken creed. Sadly their marriage does without the benefits of others' help. Possibly the very help that would change everything.

We flatly refuse the help all around us from those who are able to recount trials that sound surprisingly like our own. These are the compassionate witnesses who have answers, if you would let them know that you have questions, and who will offer wisdom they have gained from their own experiences. We silently suffer such devastating losses that our love for each other and our desire to continue can slowly begin to erode.

Everything you need is available but it is not always inside you. In our search for help we often overlook most potentially beneficial gifts right at hand, leaving them unwrapped in the box. Wasted treasures.

Instead, tiny but powerfully significant pieces of what you need will be available for the taking in the revealing testimony of a friend, or in the pages of a book you previously had no interest in reading, or in a bit of unsolicited advice that would never have seemed relevant to you before. Here in any of these unexpected places, or a million others, will be the seeds of a new idea about how to work out a difficulty between the two of you. Or just enough perspective to see what you hadn't noticed before, or enough gentle but firm rebuke to soften your stubborn heart, or enough encouragement to keep hoping for what is yet unseen.

You must adopt an open-eyed, open-minded receptivity and a willingness to slow down and humbly draw near to those whom you'd normally rush away from. Do so by opening your mouth and explaining exactly what troubles you, why it does, and what you sincerely want for your marriage. Simply by adding a third party to the mix you heighten the possibility of hearing a useful fresh perspective or uncovering a previously hidden root problem. Blinded by our pain, we often miss what an objective third party can see quite readily.

None of us can afford to be too snobbish or embarrassed when it comes to accepting the aid and support of others. Look closely around you and discover the wise and compassionate ministers, therapists, well-chosen friends who know you well and quite possibly know from experience what you are up against. They are not prying eyes or itching ears from which you must hide the truth about yourselves. They have become for you the very mouth of God declaring wisdom to help you build a gloriously indestructible marriage.

For the sake of your marriage,
whom do you need to reach out to this week?

The Vow of Extravagant Creativity

Whatever you did yesterday for the good of your marriage or your mate must never be considered your best effort. Pause only briefly to reflect together upon your accomplishments before striving to exceed them.

ADAM TOOK EVE TO the top of a very high mountain, where a breathtaking panorama was laid out before them. He led her to the hot springs hidden in a rocky cliff. Eve gasped with delight at what she saw. Her husband opened his kidskin pouch and sprinkled its delicate contents—lilac and jasmine petals—into the steaming waters. Gently Adam bathed his wife, then massaged her with the costly oil of myrrh for which he had traded his precious wood carvings. Then, as Eve lay in a shaded patch of lemongrass, Adam combed her hair. He fed her dates and pistachios; then Adam cradled his wife in his arms as she napped. The sun had become a fiery ball in the sky when Eve finally stirred. Adam kissed his wife softly and repeatedly, rousing her sluggish senses. "How did you dream all this up and what have I done to deserve it, my husband?" She purred and stretched languorously in his arms. Adam spoke in whispered tones to his wife, relating every word he could recall from when the Creator had tutored them in The Vow of Extravagant Creativity.

I never intended that the passage of time would cause the two of you to offer less of any good things to each other than when you first started out. Time and growing familiarity must always produce much more and much better from your love. Settling comfortably into "good enough" will never be good enough for your marriage.

After a time your marriage is likely to experience some tiny, at first nearly imperceptible, shrinkage. Where early on you always offered fully detailed answers, you now give a bare-bones response. Before, your good-byes always included a lingering kiss and a passionate embrace. It has now shrunk to a quick, friendly pat on the back or a ritual dry peck on the cheek. And your previously wide and uncontrollable smile when your mate enters the room has shrunk to a bland half-nod of recognition. It is just enough; not worthy of any complaint, yet hardly worth noting either.

Shrinkage is seldom connected to any serious crisis in your marriage. When serious upheaval, such as hostility, mistrust, long-unresolved conflict, or angry indifference are present, you are more likely to terminate, not subtly reduce, your daily expressions of intimacy and affection. Shrinkage means offering your mate nothing more than what is necessary, what is adequate, after having vowed much more than that. Shrinkage to the level of "good enough" can keep two people who love each other living the mundane rather than the "much more."

Many of us subscribe to the "If it ain't broke, don't fix it" philosophy when it comes to ongoing effort in an enduring marriage. We see good times, comfort, and contentment as the time to stop applying new strategies, choosing instead to simply maintain the status quo. Do you stop eating once you have achieved good health? No, you understand that you are healthy only *because* you've been eating the right food. Likewise, the health of your marriage will depend on both your efforts to accommodate and anticipate its growth.

Return to giving yourself to your mate in the overflowing way you once did. Though now, as then, your mate has neither requested nor required that you do, I want you to choose to return to the expansive, "extra-added" version of your loving acts. Choosing to offer more than what's required is to make a commitment to extravagant creativity.

The key to ceaseless creativity in marriage lies in your determination to pay attention at all times, seeking opportunities to pioneer new and different practical expressions of your support and appreciation of your mate. Focusing on your mate's unspoken needs provides you creative caring opportunities to serve imaginatively from the place in your heart that is most vulnerable. It adds depth and substance to your union. This creativity has as its goal the continual binding of two together in mind and heart. You seek, moment by moment, strategies to make your partner feel adored. And your seeking takes you to places beyond the obvious where you will heal unseen pain and expose the as-yet undeveloped strengths of your relationship. Creativity makes something from nothing.

Familiarity, mindless habits, and the endless demands of your lives will tempt you to conserve your resources wherever you can. You will unconsciously and innocently shave off bits of time and effort from your former expressions of lavish loving to transfer that energy to other areas of your life where you operate at a deficit. And since your beloved has voiced no complaint and since you definitely haven't completely stopped expressing your love, the individual shrinkage can go unnoticed. That is, until it is so obvious that your marriage begins to feel boring and increasingly mundane, and no longer the source of refreshment and delight it once was.

Never believe that what you did yesterday for your marriage, your mate, or your future together is a finished work. You must take only the briefest pause to reflect on what you have accomplished and consider how you will build on that. A couple that won't look ahead will always circle back to what was, attempting to reap the same benefits, the same resources, and the same answers for changing circumstances, different questions, and evolving needs. To keep aiming for the extravagant is to continuously pursue fresh new opportunities to lavishly express your devotion and invest new, increasingly more potent personal resources into your relationship.

Deliberately express affection and adoration above and beyond the call of duty, and in spite of the long passage of time. Decide to make visible and tangible what you know in your heart—that your mate is a rare treasure, a gift, and worth treating as such. Extravagant creativity keeps us on our toes, stretching ourselves toward more and better. Every expression of it will reaffirm to your mate the value he or she holds to you. Your continuing efforts declare that you are by no means finished reminding your mate of your delight in sharing this life with him or her. Consider what you might gain when outlandish extravagance becomes your minimum.

What would your mate say is your proudest strength as a husband or wife? How might you yet improve upon it?

The Vow of Assured Adequacy

Any attempt to achieve your personal identity and self-worth from your marriage will inevitably prove futile. Your value is an already established fact.

"I ADMIRE HOW THEY WORK their field together," said Eve as she and Adam observed their neighbors tending to their grape arbors. "I have invited you to join me in the fields so many times, but you always refuse," said Adam. "Yes, but you have never made me feel as if I could do a good job there," Eve shot back with an accusing tone that surprised both of them. "Eve, you must gain your *own* confidence by going to the fields and working hard. I cannot give it to you." There had been several such exchanges like this between them since the beginning. The Man felt as if the only way Eve could be proud of her abilities was through his constant verbal affirmations. It was too overwhelming a burden. No matter how many times he complimented her on her work, or asked her to join him in the fields, it was never enough. Eve thought he was always being condescending or simply placating her. Adam felt frustrated and unappreciated; Eve, unaffirmed and insecure. Both had had enough of each other's feelings by the time The Creator came across the fields toward them. When He arrived, without even a greeting, God began to instruct them in The Vow of Assured Adequacy.

Why do you look to your mate for what I have already given you? You can only know your significance by seeing yourself as I see you. I am neither blind to, nor repulsed by, your weaknesses. Neither am I overly impressed by your strengths. I know the truth about you. You are worthy and complete to Me because I say you are—in light of and in spite of what I know about you. I have the authority to create and call it good. You are My treasured handiwork, the purposeful expression of My own desires and intentions. If you could see what I see when I look upon you, you'd need no other validation. By whose appraisal are you validating your significance?

Being married will not give you a sense of significance any more than it will give you a second set of legs. Any attempt to gain your sense of personal worth from any relationship or achievement will prove futile. Your value is an already established fact. It is a spiritual reality that has been predetermined by God, whether it *feels* true or not.

I recently heard Julia Roberts's thoughtful response to a talk show host who asked if the star felt she was worth the multi-million-dollar paycheck she receives for each film. Roberts's answer was profound. I understood her to be saying that it wasn't her feelings that determined whether she is worth it or not. The fact is paying customers at the box office had already determined that she is.

To many, marriage has become an emergency room for needy souls seeking validation and reassurance. Self-esteem has become the focus of many unions, where each partner is too concerned about his or her personal security and value to express the selfless, unconditional generosity required in all good marriages. We ignore our vows to love, honor, and cherish each other because we are so busily engaged chasing what we already possess.

You are enough. You must believe that because when you don't you desperately search for validation in your mate's every gesture and expression. In every word, you will demand confirmation of how clever or desirable or exceptional you are. When we aren't sure that we are worth it, we will beg those who love us to constantly prove our significance to them.

Your mate's actions and opinions can affect your feelings of significance, but they can neither determine nor destroy what is already true about you. To allow any human being (including your spouse) that power is to make the person carry a burden he or she cannot and *should* not be required to carry.

In what ways will you admit to seeking your significance from your marriage? Is it by a need for constant applause, perfect reciprocity, or by needing to get your way when there's conflict between you? Perhaps it's more subtle. Is your pursuit of *more* from your mate—more attention, more sympathy, more goods and services—really a demand that your mate prove to you that you're worth it?

How did you react the last time someone failed to acknowledge your most recent "completely unselfish" act? If you were angry and couldn't shake it, secretly vowing never to waste your time offering that kindness again, then your motive was not selfless devotion but the pursuit of yet more validation. As always, unless you are already assured of your adequacy apart from your spouse's appraisal, his or hers will *never* be enough.

Give up trying to get your sense of significance from your marriage or your mate. Neither was created for that. You will only buy into the reality of your significance if you know yourself as reflected in the eyes of God. Yours will be the calm assurance of a settled fact. You will be free to give your love lavishly and live your life fearlessly, having accepted your God-given significance. It was yours all along.

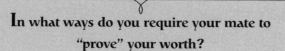

In what ways do you require your mate to "prove" your worth?

The Vow of Unreserved Devotion

It's easy for you to love excellently when all is well in your own life. It can be excruciatingly difficult to do so when the weight of your life seems too much to bear.

E DID NOT BRING THEM to the rocky cliffs often. But when He did, Adam and Eve knew The Creator wanted to teach them something important. Something that they might otherwise completely overlook. The Man and The Woman had lately experienced a stream of unexpected losses. Much of their crops had washed away in the rains. There had been a grave conflict between their sons; and Adam had been battling ill health for some time. The Creator led them upward, toward a small cove surrounded by massive boulders atop a granite plateau. "What do you see?" He asked. Adam and Eve peered inside. A mother eagle, perched precariously above her nest, was feeding her young. Eve noticed her halting movements. "She has been injured." "And yet," said Adam, "her eaglets suffer no lack." As they watched, The Man and The Woman wondered to themselves how she was able to take such care for her young when she was so weak herself. He immediately responded to their unvoiced question. "Because she has simply determined that she will. Are you willing to love like that?" Without waiting for their answer God explained to Adam and Eve The Vow of Unreserved Devotion.

To have a lasting marriage requires that you vow to give the best of all you have and all you are, even when your own personal agonies seem overwhelming and your resources have been nearly depleted. Give to the very last anyway. You need not hold back your last tiny measure of strength and resolve fearing that you will need to tend to yourself. Trust that I have sufficient power for your hurt, fatigue, and anger. Keep focused on each other's. I do not expect you to possess the might and power to pull this off on your own. It will only be accomplished by My Spirit at work in you and through you.

When Aladrian and I bought our first house we were uninitiated in the world of real estate. After a lengthy search we found a place that we fell head over heels in love with and wanted to buy. We believed we were ready to sign on the dotted line, but the conditions and requirements spelled out in fine print intimidated us. One condition of getting the loan was that we maintain a reserve account, equaling six months of mortgage payments. This, the banker explained to us, was to be sure that if Aladrian and I ever found ourselves the victims of a financial reversal there would be enough in the account to keep up our monthly obligation to them. They made it very clear to us that no matter the "what if" that might arise in our lives, that reserve could be used only for satisfying our mortgage commitment.

It is always easy to love when all is well with you. It is excruciatingly difficult to bring your best when your life or your lover is disappointing you. If you are not careful, you will confuse difficulty with impossibility and label them one and the same. And they are not.

At this very moment are you willing to offer your beloved the very best you have, *even if* . . . ? Even if you are bone-weary, bearing the exhausting demands upon you at this time? Even if you have just suffered a devastating loss or are staring at overwhelming obstacles? Even if you are in a dry season where your soul is parched and your life has suddenly become quite complicated? Will you offer the best of your attention, your patience, affection, and faithfulness to your mate, even when you aren't getting as much in return? Do not expect to find the answer by merely assessing your good intentions. Good intentions are merely lofty goals we devise, barring the emergence of unforeseen circumstances. It is naïveté, not commitment, that offers the best so long as nothing too difficult or costly or demanding occurs. But they do occur—and always when you least expect them to. Good intentions are soon found to have been flimsy hopes as long as no what ifs come up.

Don't be fooled by the kind of effort, goodwill, and positive regard that you offer your mate when your own life is progressing along joyously. It's only when you are struggling against your own personal set of harsh realities that offering your very best to your mate seems like an absurdly unrealistic objective. We'll settle for less, then label it "good enough, considering what I'm up against." "My response was kind enough, my efforts sufficient, my affection visible enough, considering how I've been treated." Or, "Under the circumstances, I could not be expected to offer any more or better than this." Your human nature rushes to tend to your own wounds and weariness, to love yourself first, to bring your best resources to the care of yourself.

But such a love is riddled with conditions and loopholes that seem to justify lowering the level of your commitment from the height of the Himalayas down to that of an anthill. From time to time there are reasons why your loving commitment *could* be less, but they must never be used as excuses for why it *should* be less.

The next time that you find yourself struggling against personal disappointments, remind yourself that though it may make giving and doing your all more difficult, you must refuse to take it as a license to lessen the bountiful flow of your demonstrated devotion.

Do you excuse yourself from the obligation to give
or do your best for your mate when you are under stress?

The Vow of Tolerance

Allowing your mate the right to his or her own "personal chaos" without punishing your partner for it.

IS THIS NOT EDEN?" protested Adam. "Was not ours a wise, divinely appointed union?" Almost daily Eve wondered aloud, "Was I wrong to expect that living here with him should include some semblance of order, some peaceful, synchronized coexistence?" The Man found himself wishing for the early days, before The Woman had come, when he could find everything exactly where he had left it. Not so, now. The Woman complained that the demands of their lives ran them frantically in too many directions—usually *opposite* directions. Where was the order, the smooth coordination of interests, responsibilities, organizing abilities, and pacing that the two had assumed would naturally occur in their marriage? They were just at the point where they had begun to weary of each other's ways. They were at the point where both did not believe they could tolerate another second of being vulnerable to their mate's disorderly way of doing things. It was at that frustrated point that God stepped in and told Adam and Eve about The Vow of Tolerance.

I have offered you My patient presence, even in the dark tumult of your sometimes scattered, chaotic lives. In love I have chosen you and I stand ready to accept you as you are—while longing to see you become so much more. I have created you with the power of choice, fully knowing that you may exercise that choice in ways that result in disorder and waste. However, I have more hope than frustration, more acceptance than frustration, more acceptance than insistence. Nothing about how you are scares Me away from you. Will you mimic Me by offering this kind of love?

On days when I am the one who retrieves our mail it is my habit to stand directly over the wastebasket where I quickly scan each piece of correspondence and immediately discard all that I consider nonessential. Aladrian complains that I throw away too much too fast. Tossing away mail that has the threatening potential to bring clutter to the top of my desk and chaos into my life appeals to my personal sense of orderliness. My wife has an altogether different approach.

On days when Aladrian retrieves the mail she piles it neatly on a well-worn corner of the hallway table until a later time that she has set aside to carefully review and process each piece. She makes a mental note to return to this pile "when I am ready to fully focus on the mail and have time to do it right." This system appeals to Aladrian's personal sense of orderliness.

When she sees me moving swiftly from the mailbox to the waste-basket she groans at what she finds quite a "disorderly" method. When I pass the hallway table and notice the leaning pile awaiting her attention, I bristle at her "disorderly" ways.

We have resigned ourselves (albeit grudgingly) to the fact that our individual approaches to achieving order are completely incompatible. We have married someone who has every right to maintain a personal sense of order—or to have none at all.

Marriage means being bonded closely enough to another person to be subject to the physical, spiritual, and psychological disarray in your mate's life. You cannot achieve marital intimacy without living within the realm of each other's brand of chaos.

We are likely to become disgusted with our spouses, maddened by what seems to us to be their odd method of organizing the various components of their lives into manageable cohesiveness. Be it their appointments, their living or work space, their health, their family relationships, or their underwear drawer, we have at times been aghast at the difference between the two of us.

Typically our first response to our mates' chaos is to offer advice. We aim to build a kindly, but persuasive argument that we feel assured our partners will appreciate and that they will promptly move to act upon. They listen, and perhaps for a time seem to agree with our assessment. Yet, in the end, they go about arranging their affairs in their old familiar way. In our growing frustration we may then become their "therapist," insightfully pointing out to them how their chaotic ways are harmful to them. That failing, we go on to become their conscience's inner voice, aiming to make them feel guilty for making us feel so discomfited by their disorder. Then we challenge them to change and prescribe a cure sure to help them do so: that they become like us. And when they fail to comply, we view their "insistence" of living life their way as "proof" that they really don't value our feelings at all.

What really bugs us is that their right to do it their way means we can never have complete control of the orderliness and appearance of the space that we inhabit. The one we married, who is in many ways unlike us, is always making choices that affect what our world looks like. That kind of vulnerability can stir up at least a little resentment in the best of us.

Unchecked resentment eventually triggers our most intense response yet: withdrawal.

In a desperate last-ditch attempt to remove ourselves from our mate's personal disarray, we distance ourselves from each other. We are convinced it is not justifiable but essential to preserving our sanity. So the dividing up begins. Your part of the room/my part of the room. Your part of our money/my part of our money. Your friends/my friends. My property/your property. It does bring us a measure of control again, but only by forfeiting intimacy, the shared life that we chose marriage over singleness for in the first place.

Instead, commit to a kind of love where you share your preferences and suggestions, then gracefully accept (endure) however much or little of it your mate changes on account of it. Refuse to pass judgment upon your spouse's way of handling his or her own affairs. Living in close proximity to someone else's unorganized, disorderly ways of being can at times be maddening. But tolerating your partner's right to his or her chaos and choosing not to allow it to drive you apart from each other is the kind of profoundly practical commitment upon which indestructible marriages are built.

> **W**hen you are absolutely certain that your way is the "right" or better way, what makes you so sure?

The Vow of Confession

The bold, dangerous commitment to let yourself be seen as you really are, when you could have kept your unsightliness hidden from your mate's view.

ADAM HAD SEEN ONE OF the other wives bathing beneath a secluded waterfall. Not just seeing her; he intently watched her. When the woman saw Adam, she did not move to cover herself immediately. They shared the briefest moment of forbidden pleasure. It was as harmless as the other flirtations that Adam had lately begun to enjoy. Still, deep within The Man knew that it was a moment that should never have happened. He was certain Eve would never find out if he simply kept these isolated instances to himself. After all, nothing had happened or would happen, he reasoned. "Why should I hurt her unnecessarily?" he asked himself aloud. At that moment, a flood of guilt washed over him and he knew he was not alone. He knew as well that his secrets were growing too large to be kept back from his wife. And as God accompanied a shaken Adam on the long walk home, He revealed to him the unlikely benefits of The Vow of Confession.

My most tender compassion swells in response to your simple and sincere acknowledgment that you have faltered. Ours is a worthless love if I cannot count on you to speak your shameful secrets and you cannot count on Me to love you beyond what was spoken. Ultimately, confession means that I matter to you. For in confessing, you call unholy what I have declared unholy. And you give Me the chance to prove that My love is made of more than mere words. I treasure every opportunity to affirm My love to you. Confession is the dark, dangerous pathway to the center of your most profound grace and love for each other.

The element of your humanity that resists confession makes a persuasive threat: *"Confessing my sins may expose me to blame and ridicule."* True. *"Acknowledging my faults may leave me without affection, alone, or ashamed."* True. Yet, in the face of one million intimidating reasons to deny your guilt, rather than declare it, *confess* to each other.

It is outrageous to risk such vulnerable exposure. But building you into a bond of love means forging a bond of truth. I know, it is uncharted territory. You think, "What harm will a little white lie do?" "What good will it do to tell him and hurt him?" You must not only recognize each other's flawless qualities, but your heartless acts, your petty motives, and your failed integrity as well. For only when you entrust these to the mercy of another are you able to be truly known and loved, truly forgiven and truly reconciled.

Confession is an opportunity, a bold, dangerous opportunity, to be seen as you are when you could have kept your unsightly parts hidden from your mate's view. Confession is an opportunity to receive a pardoning embrace. And even greater than this, to give the respect of truth telling is to prove that your beloved matters more to you than your feelings do. It is the acknowledgment that you were a wrongdoer; and, that your mate is worthy of hearing, in your words, and seeing, in your contrite expression, that your greatest pain is not because of your own shame, but because of your mate's hurt.

Now you do not need to go scavenging through the past to unearth what has been forgotten. Your marriage is not made better by the numbers of your admissions. *Sufficient unto each day is the evil thereof.* Start with today and every today hereafter. Name the failure and call it wrong with no equivocation or justification. Do it the moment that you become aware that you have failed the one you love. Procrastination is only a search for an easier, softer way. Of course there is none.

Do not require reciprocity as a condition of your own confession. Your mate's faults may hang ominously in the air, seen but never acknowledged. You must not allow that to hinder the flow of your own. Sincere confession offers the virtues of humility, integrity, and character. There are no greater gifts that you will offer in the name of love.

Have you experienced any connection between
a refusal to confess your faults and feelings
of loneliness in your marriage?

The Vow of Voluntary Amnesia

To have been gravely disappointed by your mate and to choose, over time, to treat the experience as forgotten is an unpopular choice, an outrageous commitment thoroughly infused with grace.

EVE FINALLY CAME TO a stop. She breathed deeply, taking in the pungent scent of the sage shrubs that lined the path. Angry and frustrated, she had wandered aimlessly for hours, completely oblivious to everything but the thought of what Adam had done. "How dare he? I'll never forget it as long as I live." The Creator greeted her with a kiss just behind her ear. "Why are you hiding, Eve?" She turned away, as if to shield her eyes from the sun. "How can I be hiding if you've found me?" "Oh, but you're not hiding from Me. You're hiding from him." He pointed to a clearing just ahead where Adam stood, watching, but trying not to. The sight of him brought it all back to her. A glassy wall of unshed tears threatened to break their invisible dam. "I'll never forget what he did as long as I live!" she protested. He held The Woman close as if He had the intention of never letting her go. Finally God beckoned The Man to join them. Then, in a near-whisper that both Adam and Eve could hear completely, He began to explain The Vow of Voluntary Amnesia.

The two of you, and all of humankind, are full of a mix of sincerity and rebellion, meticulousness and sloth, earnestness and carelessness, faithfulness and fear. I do not continue to lavish My love on you because you have never betrayed, abandoned, or offended Me. Nor is it because your failings do not matter to Me. No, I have noticed your acts of selflessness and I do not forget them. I have also noticed your acts of callous disregard. But I choose to bury your failures deep in the murky waters of My forgetfulness. It is to this kind of voluntary amnesia that I call you. Be assured, I am not dull-witted, unable to recognize right from wrong. Neither am I blind. It is only that I do not pile up your past offenses to hold them against you forever. I refuse to treat them as reasons to punish

you more severely when you fail in the future. Each of your failings stands alone. Each, whether one of many or of a few, is eligible for My limitless grace and utter forgetfulness. Never forget that I am the truest model of love, and the most unforgettable thing about Me is that I choose voluntary amnesia in My dealings with you. Marriage will daily provide you the opportunity to follow My example, or to completely ignore it.

We dread being forgetful. What we deem important we also consider unforgettable. We tend to our endless lists that remind us what must be done. And it is agony to discover, far too late, that something important slipped our minds. Consider how accomplished you feel when, just in the nick of time, you remember something you believed you could not afford to forget, but had.

Aladrian and I have not always been models of perfection to each other. Our early days of starry-eyed bliss and romantic declarations of our heartfelt commitment may have duped us into believing that we would never, under any circumstances, fail each other. Now we know better. In countless ways we have wronged each other. At times it was inadvertent, when we weren't paying sufficient attention to each other's needs or our opportunities to meet them. At other times it was intentional, when our insecurity, impatience, or a taste for vengeance got the better of us. Every time it did, our heart's longing was for our trespass to be forgiven, but beyond that—utterly forgotten.

You have come to view negative experiences, such as shabby treatment, an unkind remark, an insensitive act, an overwhelming betrayal, as matters of supreme importance. You cling to your memories, fearing that you'll pay a huge price in the future if you don't remember that awful thing that happened yesterday—or years ago.

Of course it will only make it harder for you to move on, informed by the past, but not shackled to it.

Something makes us think we must catalogue every detail for future reference. To turn the cliché into a commitment and choose to forgive and forget leaves us vulnerable to what we all dread most: *The Next Time*. Understandably neither of you ever wants there to be one.

It could make you feel foolish. Caught unawares, incapable of delivering yourself from the threat of being wronged again. Maintaining a readily accessible record of each other's every transgression seems like wisdom essential to your own survival.

Electing to forget does indeed make you vulnerable. Those with perfect memories get started right away setting protective strategies so as not to be hurt again. Fearful human nature always tends to be heavy-handed when it comes to self-protection. More always seems better than less. Even though the more self-protective you are the more self-centered you are likely to become. One cannot love ably when one's focus is turned completely selfward.

Forgive each other's transgressions. But do not deny them. It is a superficial, misguided amnesia that prematurely dismisses trespasses. It is not motivated by anything as pure as grace, mercy, or forgiveness, but by fear. Fear fashions a world of illusion where hear no evil, speak no evil, see no evil is a gesture that smacks of artifice.

Such denial is only an anesthesia, not a remedy. Amnesia is a commitment to mercy. Mercy is an irrelevant concept when there is no guilt present. You have, in fact, wronged each other. You will again. Stand ready to forget what has been acknowledged as wrong. First having made every effort to determine the origins of the failure and the practical means to avoid it in the future. Never rush to offer a shallow mercy that is not based on painful examination and mutual acknowledgment of the offense. Name the offense to the one you love. Complain about its hurtfulness. Call for an accounting. Hear the confession. Accept the apology. Stand ready to forgive everything.

Choose to forget all that has been sincerely and adequately dealt with. Then, and only then, should you exile it to the faraway recesses of your fading memory.

Treat your mate and yourself as one who always has the capacity to fail again, but as one who is not condemned for having failed in the past.

Impossible, you say. Vow to do it and it will become possible as you go.

In what secret ways do you work to ensure that you don't forget your mate's past offenses toward you?

The Vow of Contentment

The stern refusal to believe that life or love is obligated to meet your complete satisfaction.

ADAM ALWAYS LOOKED FORWARD TO his time alone with The Creator. He could speak freely, without fear of being misunderstood or repeatedly having to explain what he meant by every word. With Him, Adam never felt as though he had to prove anything. The Man hated admitting it, but spending time with God most appealed to him because it was time away from Eve. "Adam, I sense some unrest in you." The Man used to find God's probing nature unsettling; now, however, he appreciated His directness. "I guess I'm thinking about Eve and me," he said. "You know I love her, but I often wonder why I couldn't have someone more cooperative and far less critical. Why did you choose marriage for me at all? I see some of the young men who are without wives. Their lives seem more suited to my independence." Adam fully expected his remarks to be met by utter silence, The Creator's usual response to these kinds of outbursts from Adam. Instead He spoke immediately, explaining to The Man The Vow of Contentment.

There are sure dangers in your discontent. Never believe, not even for a moment, that life must serve you only what completely satisfies you. To be content is a choice you make, a choice to accept as sufficient for the kind of marriage you have without giving up your vision for it to be more than it is now. You have committed yourselves to each other for better or for worse. I have committed Myself to giving you the strength to fulfill that promise. Choose to be content—never complacent, but always content— with what you have today. Then by faith, believe that I can deliver you and marriage into a kind of tomorrow that is infinitely better than your today.

As often as I can I drive down the road from our home to my favorite "quiet place"—a secluded pond hidden in a small park full of dozens of olive and eucalyptus trees. There is a gaggle of hospitable ducks that play among the pond's water lilies, with their stunningly pink blossoms. When I am at the pond I am content. My life is fine as it is when I am seated there on the tiny boat dock with my feet dangling over the edge, my toes tickling the water. It is my pond and when I am there I am absolutely content.

None of this is because my quiet place is without it imperfections. At times, after a rain, my pond turns a murky brown color. Gnats buzz annoyingly to distract me, and now-departed visitors have left cigarette butts and fast-food wrappers strewn about. Still, this is the place that I have chosen to contemplate its glories and to accept its flaws. Here I have *decided* to be content. Here I experience the fact that contentment is a decision to train my eyes more upon what is truly good about where I am instead of all that's bad there.

Over the long course of your marriage there will seem to be at times, another place, another feeling, another person, that will seem much better suited for you than the one you already have. You'll see, or think you see, another picture of marriage that will seem so much more inviting than the one you've built for yourself. Beyond inviting, it will seem absolutely ideal. The way it should have been for you in the first place. The option that, had you known then what you know now, would have been your choice. The more you concentrate on this supposedly ideal situation, the more you will feel assured that whom and what you have now is not only less desirable, but is so emotionally unsatisfying that it constitutes an injustice.

As you take your continued comfort in the fantasy, you will grow to despise individual pieces of your real-life marriage, and your real-life partner, deeply unsettled by the absolute unfairness and futility of your present circumstances. You can't possibly focus on what your marriage can be if you remain obsessed with what it isn't or with how much greener the grass could be (or would have been) "over there."

A neighbor, Marcus, has been married for more than sixteen years. In their second year he had a brief but intense extramarital affair that almost cost him his marriage. Now, with many years of hindsight, Marcus pulls no punches when he explains the slow, discontented progression that led to his unfaithfulness. "I started making this mental list of what I wasn't getting out of my wife and my marriage. As the list got larger it was easy to forget all the good that I was getting. Then you lose your mind and make the dumbest choices."

"Over there" is an illusion. It is a cunning, three-dimensional, beautifully decorated illusion that seduces discontented spouses to fall deeply in love with it. To buy into it is to believe that the woman really was sawed in half, or that the rabbit's home really is the hat. It is to trudge toward the mirage while trampling true treasures.

Placing confidence in your suppositions about what or who would be better for you is both arrogant and self-sabotaging. Once we believe our own fantasy of how the past would have been *if only*, how the present should be *if only*, and how the future could be *if only*, we feel as if we have the right to force that fantasy into reality. Then, mind, body, and soul, you will begin to slowly disengage from your mate and your marriage and the daily opportunity you have to add new value to it. You can't bring the best of yourself to your real marriage while en route to the fantasy one. In the end only the one you nourish will survive.

It is heartbreaking to see a husband indulge a sexual fantasy that does not involve the one he says he loves. Or when a wife looks with disdain on her partner because he has failed to transport her to a state of emotional bliss, like a former lover surely would have, *if only* she had married him. Allowing your regrets to get the best of you exposes you to the threat of mutual mistrust.

Perhaps it is dramatic to suggest that by indulging your dissatisfactions you attack your spouse and violently assault your marriage. Your behavior is determined by the beliefs and perceptions inside you. Do you really believe you can abandon someone in your heart of hearts and your absence will not be felt by the person—while still sleeping in the same bed?

Dissatisfaction grows on its own from the seeds of disappointment and unrealistic comparisons. Contentment grows from determined effort. It is the result of practiced thankfulness and repeated expressions of gratitude. It is choosing to find what is good and praiseworthy in everything—your circumstances, your trials, and especially your partner. It is embracing your commitment to your marriage and your mate and treating that as the floor of your reality.

Contentment declares your mate more valuable than circumstances and pledges you to devote yourself to seeking the best in her or him, and allowing the circumstances to conform to your devotion, not the other way around. Contentment does more than look for a silver lining. It sees the clouds as harbingers of refreshing and restoring rain, occasional conflict and disappointment as opportunities to see into the heart of the one you love. Contentment is the assurance that God is willing and able to build into your marriage something more precious than the most satisfying opportunities you feel certain are available to you elsewhere.

Begin by acting as if the life you have now, the love you have now, is better than any other that might otherwise be available to you. Ask for what you want from your mate. Unless you are being cruelly treated, be ready to live (lovingly so) with what you get. Decide that any yearnings that undermine your commitment to your spouse are not an option. Ask yourself, if this fantasy were to leave my heart and become real right now, in front of my mate, would it build him or her up or tear the person down? How would it make my mate feel? Pay attention to what you have and how you can make it better. Pay more attention to what it is than what it isn't.

How much effort do you expend reflecting on what your marriage could have been (but isn't) or what it must become before you'll consider it acceptable?

The Vow of Asking

The idea of our spouse discerning and meeting our needs without our having to tell them is quite appealing to us. The only problem is that their love and commitment to us doesn't make them able to read our minds.

THE CREATOR FOUND EVE sitting alone by the river's edge. She turned to acknowledge Him. Her expression was one of defeat. He had seen her like this many times before. "What is it that you want, my dear?" He gently asked. The Woman sighed deeply. "I want many things and I want to get them without always having to beg for them each time," she blurted irritably. As if He did not already know, Eve chronicled her day for Him. She had to free a sheep caught in a bramble bush. Her freshly washed bed linens had fallen into a muddy creek. The children had noisily insisted she entertain them when they had become bored. To top it all off, she had discovered that much of her garden had been lunch to three hungry ferrets. The demands upon her seemed endless. God touched her lightly on her shoulder and peered deeply into her eyes, repeating: "Eve, what do you *really* want?" The Woman looked away to ponder His question before answering. "What I want is for Adam to hold me and listen to me complain. I want him to sympathize with me and offer his help. And, I want him to know this and do this . . ." The Creator broke in to finish her sentence: ". . . without your having to ask him for it." "Yes, that is exactly what I want," said Eve. They walked together in silence along the river. Not a word was spoken by either of them until well after nightfall. Then God slowly, tenderly spoke to Eve about The Vow of Asking.

Why don't you want to make your requests known? Might it be that you love the idea of being taken care of by an all-knowing mate? How annoyed you will be when you discover that I am the last of the all-knowing lovers. Neither love nor marriage mean giving over the responsibility for your well-being to another human being. When you don't ask

the one you love for what you need or want you are helping to ensure that you don't get it.

At this moment, outside the window of my writing room, a strong gust of wind is swirling through the canyon. Of course I can't actually see the wind; it is invisible. What I am absolutely certain of is its presence and power because I can see and hear the way it swirls through the trees, causing the branches to bend and sway and noisily rustling the leaves about. Just like the wind, unconditional love is invisible, only detectable to us as we see the visible effects of it. Until we hear it and see it in action it is at best only an unverified *feeling* of devotion, a pleasant mood, a private flush of sincerity known only to the one in whose heart it is hidden.

To some, the definitive test of a marriage's strength is being able to get the love they want, the way they want it, without their ever having to ask for it. Obviously there are certain loving acts that are rightly expected by any mate, in any marriage. They are the absolutes: to care, to communicate, to settle discord, to forgive, to listen, to respect, and a well-known host of others. Still, in actual practice, your mate is greatly helped by knowing exactly what does and does not fulfill those "universal laws" in loving you. That is where you will need to make specific requests. Even though you may wish that your mate already knew.

It is unfair to hold your spouse responsible for discerning your personal desires without your having to specifically verbalize them. Because when you truly believe that he or she should have already known, then, in your eyes, your mate is already guilty of willful disregard. None of us, even the most long-suffering, can stomach willful disregard very well.

But what if she didn't fulfill your wish because she didn't know?

And what if he didn't know because you didn't ask? If you are sure your spouse should know and shouldn't have to ask, then it is easy to leap to the conclusion that he or she didn't care. Of course, "didn't care" feels very much like "doesn't love." That possibility provokes hurt and anger in anyone.

It is a natural human tendency to want to hand over the burden of responsibility to someone you trust. Who better, we conclude, than the mates who say they love us unconditionally, for better or for worse, until death parts us? The only problem is that profound love and sincere commitment don't make your spouse able to read your mind. Even when the person directly asks what your preferences and desires are, it can be difficult to put into words. No matter your past experiences, in marriage you must now dare to believe that there is someone beside you who wants to know what you want, and wants to do something about it. Or you must finally give yourself permission to ask, even though at first you may feel embarrassingly needy or demanding to do so. One of the scripture's most bluntly stated verses declares *"You have not because you ask not. . . ."*

Of course, asking does leave you vulnerable to the very real possibility that your request will be denied, ignored, or misunderstood. There are so many reasons to remain in the safety of unexpressed desires, but there is one practical reason to make your request known that overrides them all: the seeds of resentment grow and flourish in the soil of your unfulfilled desires. When you remain silent about what you want you are sure to get less of it than you might otherwise. I want you to ask so that when you receive your request, you'll know where to direct not only your gratitude but your next request as well.

Is there anything you're expecting from your mate that you are still silently waiting for him or her to figure out on his or her own?

The Vow of Accountability

Often major discord between spouses centers on financial and material rights and privileges—who has them, and who does or does not deserve to have more of them. Unmerited generosity exorcises the spirits of greed and possessiveness.

EVE HAD BARELY SPOKEN all evening. Adam could see the stiff outline of her jaw as she stared upward, watching the cloud-filled sky give way to a furious swirl of orange, red, and gold, finally allowing the first evening stars to appear. "We should get ready for bed, my love. Tomorrow will be a very long day," he whispered behind her, as he gently embraced her. "Perhaps you should sleep with the money changer in the marketplace. He knows more of our business than I do," Eve said as she angrily removed herself from his arms. The Man's eyes fell. How had she found out? He had found a magnificent pearl in the sands near the water's edge and hidden it from his wife. After much haggling he had sold the treasure to the money changer but had not yet decided how he would spend the money. Now Adam was painfully aware that the decision was never his to make alone. The Man reached for her hands. He could summon no words of defense, only of apology. Long before Adam had finished speaking, or Eve had gotten over her anger, The Creator came to speak to them concerning The Vow of Accountability.

I care deeply about what makes you anxious. Even when you don't know what is at the root of your anxieties, I do. I have always known that it would be an exceedingly great challenge to you, to have to live in a world where poverty, deprivation, and the incessant cravings to have more plague you. You will always seek an anchor to cling to, one that will assure you that you will have sufficiency in a world where the looming question is "Will there be enough?" It is a miracle to have the two of you in charge of one pool of riches. Join together and do what mere mortals dread: surrender all that you treasure to each other.

Marriage is meaningless if it does not involve voluntarily subjecting yourselves to each other's hands in your cash box. It can be more than a little intimidating to have to give an account of what *you* have earned, how *you* want to use it, and suffer the fact that your mate will at times have a wholly different idea about it.

In marriage there is always another who has expectations and a degree of control as well as motive and opportunity to affect what happens with your material possessions.

Whether we admit it or not, all of us tend to gravitate toward a realm where we are autonomous, where we can abide by our own set of rules. Where no one else's opinions or preferences or demands can hinder us from getting what we want, the way we want it. We all claim we want ever-increasing spiritual intimacy with our mates; but to have it means revealing the truth about ourselves, including, and especially, truth that may not be visible to the naked eye. We resist the practical intimacy where mundane matters, like our money and what we do with it, are treated as corporate rather than individual concerns. Enduring your mate's scrutinizing gaze over every inch of your naked body may be easier than throwing open your ledger books and your secret shopping list. For better or for worse, where your treasure is, so too is your heart.

These days I have found that much of the ill will between husbands and wives is around ownership rights and privileges—who has them, and who does or does not deserve to have more. Where there has been greed and mistrust, we are naturally inclined to impose more rules and a stricter division of personal rights and possessions. Sharing, unmeasured generosity, and the use of the possessive pronoun *ours* are abandoned in order to serve either your lust for more material goods or your chronic fear that you might be taken advantage of. It is a sure sign that you do not have a real marriage yet—a partnership of sorts, an "arrangement," a joint tenancy, but not a marriage.

It is the love of money and the fear of the unforeseen that make husbands and wives demand their personal right to make significant financial decisions apart from each other, and to resist (often in the most subtle, passive-aggressive ways) having to answer to anyone else about it. It is not the exercise of personal liberties or the pursuit of simple convenience that drives us to such heavy-handed privacy, but the accumulated personal "baggage" containing our most secret fears and greed.

Having to answer and to agree means having to slow down your forward momentum toward your own material desires and ambitions, leaving them subject to your spouse's input and the risk that the fulfillment of your desires may be challenged, delayed, or worse— vetoed. This is insufferable to those of us who believe we should be able to make independent decisions and expect complete endorsement of those decisions by our mates.

Slow down to the more deliberate pace of generosity and accountability. Reveal your secrets, the wreckage of your financial past, your present habits, idiosyncrasies, and vulnerabilities around money. It will be well worth it even if it threatens your sense of freedom to spend it, lend it, or save it, when and where you like.

What do you fear you'd lose if you gave your mate open access to all your material and financial treasures (and full disclosure about them)? What do you hope you might gain from it?

The Vow of Small Things

Modest but frequent gestures of affection and care may individually appear slight and inconsequential, but grouped together over days and years they become the undeniable evidence of your highest love and deepest devotion.

EVE STRETCHED OUT ON the cool grass and let nature minister its most luxuriant bath to her senses. It was her birthday, and Adam had determined to make it unforgettable. "What shall I do to pay tribute to you, my love?" She smiled. His earnest expression delighted her even more than his words. "By just being, my darling. Just being Adam, right here beside me, is more than enough." Adam persisted. "Shall I pick all of the gardenias in Eden to make perfume for you? Shall I carve your name upon the face of Mount Hermon? Shall I slay a dozen leopards to make you a gown?" "No, none of those, my darling husband," Eve said gently. "Only let me breathe you close and hear my name upon your lips and wrap my body with your arms. These alone shall make me quite happy." Adam was deflated. Her requests seemed so insignificant to him. "But Eve, I am offering to do something grander than I have ever done for you before." At that moment The Creator came to speak to them both concerning The Vow of Small Things.

The bond that exists between you and Me is not established only by awe-inspiring miracles but by the tiny favors I spring upon you. I refuse to reduce our relationship to dramatic rescues and impressive displays of My power. I bring the small blessings you treasure but could do without, because My love for you compels me to seek any and every possible opportunity to express it. I take nothing for granted. I build great marriages with small things. Everything around you, in all its splendor, was created with a word. I call forth light and from that came sight, colors, sunsets, and the brilliance of diamonds. You exist because I used a small handful of earth to shape you. In fact, our relationship hinges on a tiny but oft-repeated promise: I love you.

Perhaps more than anyone, marriage partners need to remember the worth and beauty of small things—the tiny, seemingly insignificant gestures that often go unnoticed by long-married spouses. It is through these consistent blushes of tender selflessness that your and your mate's aloneness is penetrated and may eventually be dispelled. Company-keeping becomes trusted, joyous companionship, passion becomes an undeniable oneness, and the unseverable cord of intimacy is woven into your marriage.

Grand gestures say, "I choose to care about you." But the tiny acts of generosity, the briefest words of reassurance, the unexpected caress, an admiring glance, the unsolicited offer of assistance, a hand held, a whispered endearment—these tiny offerings loudly say, "You matter to me." Grand-scale displays of affection require extraordinary means and unusual opportunity. Small tokens of affection require little more than choosing to say yes to one of countless daily opportunities. Give in to the part of you that would stop to show a tender kindness if you weren't in such hasty transit to grander obligations.

The final week before I was due to turn in the completed draft of my last book was extremely stressful. Along with the anxiety deadlines always stir in me are the inevitable computer glitches (stubbornly slow printers, disappearing chapters, and the unfamiliar hieroglyphics that show up on the screen right where intelligible words once were).

Under this kind of pressure, Aladrian saw me become a preoccupied shadow presence in our home. I was totally unaware of her and seldom offered any more than an occasional monosyllabic response to her inquiries as to my progress.

Ever generous with her time, Aladrian offered to help. Did I need her to "decode" my scribbling from my yellow legal pads and onto the computer? Did I want her to meticulously proofread every page and correct the countless typos hiding there? Or would I be better served by her canceling all her appointments that day so she could stay near me for moral support?

Any of these would have been enormous sacrifices of her time and impressive demonstrations of her love for me; but at the height of my anxiety and fatigue, none of them would have meant as much to me as the one tiny, perfect gesture of her affection that she performed. Aladrian simply knelt down, removed my shoes, and silently, tenderly massaged my feet, then got up and went about her business. It was a small thing, yet I have never felt more loved and less alone than at that unforgettable moment.

As you build a life together, over time, it will be your appreciation for the small things that is most likely to be overlooked. Your oversight may not destroy what you have built, but it forfeits the opportunity to build more. The precarious balance of life's joys versus its burdensome demands will propel you toward the grand and dramatic efforts, done at appointed intervals. Your acts may be impressive, but they may speak only of your sense of duty, rather than your sense of spontaneity and generosity. You must cling to the commitment of continually making small offerings. It is these that you will give and never miss, but if not given your mate will always hunger for them.

Now turn and bless each other with your modest favors and I promise you a marvelous thing will happen. The more you give them, the more you'll recognize and appreciate them when they are returned. You and your mate will discover the pleasant challenge of finding new ways to give until these tender exchanges become a part of you.

What small gestures of affection or kindness
did you previously display but seldom, if ever, do now?

The Vow of Solitude

To many of us, the idea of solitude seems too much like *iso-lation*, a thoroughly unappealing concept that would confirm there is something wrong with our marriage. In fact, solitude is the beneficial reminder that each of you must bear up under some of the weight of your life on your own.

HE MAN AND THE WOMAN stopped beneath the olive tree to spy. An inseparable pair of macaques could always be found there perched on a low-hanging branch. Side by side, with gentle determination, the animals were grooming each other in an impressive display of perfectly synchronized movement. Adam and Eve marveled at their ability to tend to each other so completely, without a sound uttered between them. "I envy them," said Eve. "There is nothing either of them ever has to face without the other beside him." "Yes. Would that it were like that with us," Adam said, unable to hide the unmistakable hint of both disappointment and longing in his voice. Then He appeared and explained to them The Vow of Solitude.

There is no degree of intimacy in marriage that will ever completely remove your longing. There is no act of tenderness, no sympathetic response, no meaningful conversation, no display of affection, no amount of time that will completely remove this facet of your humanity. I have purposed it this way. Loneliness is one of My bittersweet gifts to you. A surprising treasure hidden beneath the sand in your driest desert. At times you must walk alone so that you become freshly acquainted with the reality of what you lack within yourself, but have in abundance in Me: My lavish love, the unfailing consistency of My presence, and the unique nature of My character and My ways. Loneliness means so much negativity to you. It means so much opportunity to Me.

We are never truly alone. Yet at times we are intimately acquainted with the pangs of loneliness. Marriage is no sure antidote for it. You will feel it most when you must face certain personal circumstances or decisions that you and your mate do not hold in common. They are yours and yours alone. Or it is in those fleeting moments when you are deeply touched, moved to tears or laughter or amazement by something that was of no interest whatsoever to your spouse. Or when you have in some way failed and must now look within yourself—not your circumstances and not your partner—to answer why.

It is at these times, even in a healthy marriage, that you are reminded that though the two of you may be united as one, you are still individuals with separate feelings, yearnings, burdens, and challenges that are yours to experience. It is there that you will find yourself startled by the binding grip of loneliness. To many of us solitude is a thoroughly unappealing concept. We see it as an alarming indication that there is something wrong with us, our mates, or our marriages. In fact, it is only the harmless reminder that each of you must bear up under some of the weight of your life on your own.

For the sake of the one you love, and your life together, make peace with your feelings of loneliness. Abandon every insistence that your mate work to say or do or be and give what you feel will banish your loneliness quickly and forever. Your pangs of loneliness must not always be followed by a demand for relief from your mate. It is an invitation to solitude for you alone. And when you have quieted your tantrums and ceased your stubborn resistance, when you have accepted passage on a solitary journey through the valley of the shadows, you will find that your ability to tolerate *by-yourselfness* is one of the greatest gifts you can bring to your union.

By the end of our weeklong honeymoon Aladrian and I had grown quite fond of being inseparable twenty-four hours a day. We shared every meal together and strolled arm in arm along the beach at both sunrise and sunset. Nearly every word we spoke for seven whole days was spoken to each other. We had shut the rest of the world out and, in each other's constant company, became matched bookends. No longer did either of us think of ourselves as "*I.*" Now there was only "*Us.*"

Naïvely we returned home expecting that a proper married life meant we continue this way. And at first it was quite easy to do so.

We conversed by phone several times a day, then rushed home from work each evening to each other's waiting arms. We declined several invitations to socialize with friends and put our hobbies and personal interests on indefinite hold.

Thinking it was the sure path to ever-increasing intimacy, we had given up virtually all our independent pursuits and private times of solitude. We had little of our day-to-day lives to share with each other because we had lived it almost entirely in each other's company. Not surprisingly we soon began to feel as if we were chained and shackled to each other and on the verge of being smothered by each other's constant presence.

We had gone too far and we knew it. We needed to get away from each other at least some of the time to be able to have something to offer each other when we were together. We acknowledged personal solitude as a benefit to our marriage, not the enemy of it. We went out and got our lives back—some separate friendships, activities, and interests that didn't require our mate's involvement for them to be considered viable. And without going overboard into isolation from each other, we each renewed our commitment to getting some time alone.

Coming home to each other soon became a delight again as we relieved each other of the burden of filling each other's lives with all the joy we could stand.

It is a false promise that a loving marriage and a devoted mate will nurture and sustain every part of your being at all times. Only God can make and keep such an extravagant promise. And you will only seek it from God after you have exhausted your attempts to find it elsewhere.

If you do not become overly distracted trying to escape its grip, there is so much you will gain in submitting to your loneliness. Keener discernment, the courage to take action, or the patience to wait. The true origins of your fears and your angers, and the true source of your bold decision to give and receive love unselfishly, unconditionally, without having to save yourself. These virtues and so many more are available only when you stop demanding—even for a moment—that life or the one you love always makes you feel embraced, joyous, or whole. To a great extent these are all richly acquired by those who are able to make themselves quite at home in solitude.

Once you grasp this, you will strangely find yourself embracing your lonely seasons, rather than insisting that your mate "fix" your feelings. You'll take responsibility for them yourself and in doing so you'll begin to develop the kind of steely self-reliance that liberates your mate from the oppressive demands of seeing to your emotional well-being. You'll become the kind of person who *needs* no one— including your spouse—to make your life easier, more exciting, or less challenging. You will emerge with fewer demands of your mate and yourself, and you will experience a near-overwhelming gratitude for your beloved, the one whom you treasure with all your heart but with not a trace of neediness.

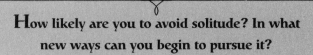

How likely are you to avoid solitude? In what new ways can you begin to pursue it?

The Vow of Unified Leadership

Committing to establish *together* the standards of right and wrong, acceptable and unacceptable–*before* holding your children accountable to them.

ADAM'S BOOMING VOICE WAS even more intimidating when he reprimanded their sons. When Eve heard it, she left her half-pressed olives and ran to the boys, but Adam turned and blocked her way. "Eve, did you tell these boys to leave their garden chores until tomorrow, after I gave them instructions to finish today?" The angry flash of Adam's eyes belied the even tone of his voice. "Yes, I did indeed!" Eve returned his stare defiantly. She thought Adam was working their sons too hard and she had meant to tell him so that morning, but an opportunity had not presented itself. "Eve, when you contradict my orders, you are telling our sons that what I say means nothing around here." Eve countered: "And when you order them about without regarding their feelings, you're telling them that my words matter even less." "You should have talked to me first," Adam snapped. "Why? So that I can get my instructions from you like the children?" Eve challenged. A loud crashing sound silenced them both when The Creator split in half the trunk of the cedar tree near their entry. "Are you *trying* to make your home as divided as that tree?" He asked angrily. With a swift gesture He ordered them to sit before Him. Then God told Adam and Eve about The Vow of Unified Leadership.

Many are the difficulties you will face together because of your secret desire to have it all go your way. Rearing children would be challenging enough alone; it is even more so when you must share the reins with someone who doesn't always see things as you do. But the marriage that has My mark upon it readily accepts the burdens of merging your individual rights, and parental authority into unified leadership. It is how your children and a doubting world will see the miracle of power and intimacy shared by two individuals, as if by one. By this you will rein-

force the strength of your partnership. Your united front will make clear to your children that whenever they obey one of you they have submitted to both of you.

Yyou will always find it simpler to exercise power when it is yours and yours alone. Sharing it calls for burdensome complications like negotiation, compromise, submission, and mutual accountability. Those who singularly wield all the power in a marriage never bother themselves with these obligations. But neither do they enjoy the benefits of equal partnership—double wisdom, strength, and experience; alternate points of view; and the multiplied strengths of shared responsibility and liability.

It is the way of your world to give more credence to power unshared. It is so self-satisfying, so uncomplicated. Each day, by watching you, your children are learning the nature of loving leadership expressed through parental authority. What's the quality of the lessons they are learning by watching the two of you?

Does one of you hide from the responsibility of making decisions and mandates that your children must submit to? Does one of you rise to make decrees without conferring with the other? Or do the two of you come after each other, revising or canceling what the other has already decreed?

Soon after getting her driver's license (and buoyed by the possibility of more independence and mobility), our eldest daughter, Corinn, found a gaping hole in our parental authority. Without conferring with each other, Aladrian and I had both set weekend curfew times for her. I had decreed midnight; Aladrian 1 A.M.

The first time Corinn returned at the later hour (awakening her parents in the process), I rose to confront her about violating "our" curfew. Aladrian rose to commend her for coming home early.

Momentarily ignoring our daughter, Mom and Dad squared off to declare our offense with each other's independent policy making. As we did, a confused and exasperated Corinn ascended the stairs to her bedroom saying, "When you two decide who's in charge here, please let me know!" Until we consulted with each other and agreed upon the time she must be home, Corinn had no time to which she absolutely had to be accountable. Understandably, when our children suspect that the rules are not important enough for their parents to discuss and agree on, then perhaps it's not so important to obey any of the rules anyway.

It is not necessary that you both require exactly the same rules and regulations of your children in every situation. Rules and regulations are simply practices enacted in submission to your principles. Practices may vary according to what either of you deems to be the most wise and strategic in a given situation. Your principles, however, must not differ. To be of one accord means that the negotiation and clarification of what will be considered right and wrong, acceptable and unacceptable, must be established between the two of you first—before you can instruct your children to submit to them. There is a wide range of ways to put most principles into practice, and you and your mate will sometimes approach them differently. To the extent that the principles are upheld by your shared authority, some of what is required or allowed of your children may vary based on which of you is there. Whichever of you it may be, you will be, at that moment, upholding your mutually established values. But neither of you must ever call for, or allow your children to do, what undermines that authority or those values.

Too much is at stake to violate this commitment. It is certain to eventually stir discord between the two of you and unclear, inconsistent policies for your children. The outcomes of such are bound to have a destructive, rippling effect through generations as your children establish their own homes according to the example set by their parents' conflict-ridden style of leadership.

This vow asks a lot of you. Frankly, it takes a good amount of your time and effort to define and agree together to the values and guiding principles that your children are expected to follow.

Unified leadership is the framework of a secure family, and the spiritual, emotional, and practical anvil upon which godly beliefs, character, and behavior are forged in your children. Begin honoring your vow to unified leadership by first establishing it as one of the highest priorities of your marriage. Daily, work to assure that you speak as with one voice; to clarify, instruct, and reestablish the solidarity of your parental leadership. To do so will be to make divine principles visible and practical to your children's children and beyond.

By observing the two of you, are your children learning that parental authority should be shared equally by both of you, or that it is held tightfistedly by one of you?

The Vow of Yielding

At times your delight will be in the actual physical and emotional gratification of lovemaking, but at other times it will be in the very act of submitting your will, your schedule, and your body to your mate's desire for you.

ADAM SLID QUIETLY into bed. He lay close to Eve, molding his body to the contours of hers. For several minutes he caressed her smooth skin downward from her shoulder to her waist to the curve of her hip. This had become his usual unspoken sexual overture. She lay motionless, feigning sleep and recalling to herself how Adam had ignored her advances two nights before. That night she had flirtatiously summoned him to bed, but he was tired and preoccupied. He had pretended that he did not catch her hint. Frustrated and angry, The Woman had finally dozed off. Now Adam's low whisper blew a warm breath just above her ear. "Eve?" He kissed her softly on her neck. A part of her very much wanted to make love with her husband. Another part of her wanted to settle the score. "No, Adam. I'm tired. Not tonight," she groaned drowsily. Then it dawned on him. She was getting revenge. He instantly removed himself to the edge of his side of the bed. He turned his back hoping to clearly convey his indifference. Adam and Eve both pulled their half of the bed linens tightly around themselves, daring not to allow the slightest slack. Over an hour passed without a word spoken between them. Then The Creator's voice broke the sleepless silence to teach them The Vow of Yielding.

Marriage, as I intended it, is the most intimate of human relationships. Sex is for you to passionately express and joyously celebrate that intimacy. Of course no mates are free to abandon themselves to something so profound when they feel they must keep a strict tally of who is most often getting his or her way. Then your sexual intimacy is really only a proving ground where you each crusade for recognition of your rights and insist that your own selfish desire—that you cleverly call "needs"—must be served.

If sex is about intimacy, then it is also about trust. Trust cannot be gained or given without yielding. Settle it within yourselves that in the area of sexual intimacy your bodies belong to each other, yours to your spouse and your spouse's to you. There is no greater physical or spiritual delight than that which comes from willingly submitting yourself to the tender care and creativity of the one you have vowed to love until death separates you.

This, of course, challenges that part of us that wants to decide the when and the how of anything that involves us. As staunch advocates of the notion of sovereign rulership of our own bodies, we think nothing of freely exercising our perceived "right to refuse." So we attempt to satisfy our thirst for power wherever we can—even in our bedrooms. The unfortunate casualty of this struggle for power is our own sexual intimacy.

We all have very definite ideas about what is the right and proper time, place, and manner to express our love for each other sexually. Those who always insist upon an extended evening of romance that builds slowly from intimate conversation to several stages of love play often are resistant to yielding themselves to a quick unplanned lovemaking that could make them a little late for an appointment. Those who favor the adrenaline-surging pleasure of spontaneous, fast-paced lovemaking are often resistant to a slower, more detailed sexual encounter.

At times your greatest delight will be in the actual physical gratification of making love; but at other times it will be in the very act of yielding your will, your timing, and your body to your mate's desire for you.

In this we are all indeed quite vulnerable. Our nakedness is not only physical, but emotional and spiritual as well. To yield is to offer your body to your mate voluntarily and unreservedly. Anything less than mutual surrender makes you each other's opponent.

You have gifts to give one another within the cloistered privacy of your home that means you trust your mate to declare your worth to you, while you set your heart on declaring his or hers. Consenting to the sexual desires of your lover affirms the value you place on your mate. So does at times yielding to a "no" when you were counting on a "yes."

Something miraculous happens when sex ceases to be about power and becomes an exercise in the surrender of power. A wall of safety is built around the two of you. Making love becomes a privilege instead of an obligation. An abiding sense of closeness becomes abundantly available without the need for harsh demands.

Have you become less or more available to your mate sexually than when you were first married?

The Vow of Relinquishment

The outrageous commitment to allow your mate to take responsibility for managing the consequences of his or her own choices.

THIS IS COLD!" Adam growled as he spat out the first mouthful of his evening meal. He had not come in from the fields at midday and was now ravenous. The Man's shoulders and back ached from tilling a hard stretch of virgin land. When he arrived home only to be greeted with this inedible gruel set before him and no fire to warm him, Eve knew this would happen. She had told Adam for several days that his wood supply was running low. When he sharply accused her of nagging, she stopped mentioning it altogether. Now he was livid. Eve continued wrapping and tying dried figs for storage. "You should have made me fetch the wood this morning, or at least reminded me again!" Adam insisted. "It was you who chose not to listen days ago, and you who chose to wait," Eve calmly replied, without looking up from her work. The Man rose from the table to protest further. Suddenly the door nearest him flew open and a cold gust of wind bit into him. The Creator had arrived. He had every intention of using this opportunity to explain The Vow of Relinquishment.

I do not create painful consequences, as much as I allow them, and make use of them for My purposes and your benefit. When you put yourself in the middle of your mate and his or her consequences, you are shielding the person from pain, but also blocking access to My redemptive work. Your misplaced sympathy can hinder vital changes in your mate that you have long hoped and prayed for. Know that I love you both too much to allow My work to be impeded by anyone. I see before you do when your mate gets into a seemingly unmanageable predicament. I alone am able to turn your foolish choices into new wisdom and maturity. Consequences are the means by which I accomplish this. Stand out of My way and relinquish your mate to My transformative hands.

Causing pain, and allowing someone to have pain, are two different things. In marriage there should be no place for deliberate contribution to any kind of suffering between you and your mate. But at all times you must get out of the way and allow your mate to face the consequences—even the painful consequences—of choices he or she has made.

Consequences are the inevitable fruit of your every decision. Though they may be harsh, they are neither revenge nor punishment. In fact the consequences of your mate's choices are seldom engineered by one act. They are more regularly the crops that are reaped from certain seeds sown ignorantly or foolishly.

It is only natural to flinch and groan along with your beloved as he or she endures the ill effects of poor choices. Every fiber of your being will be moved sometimes by compassion, at other times by guilt and the feeling that you are responsible for bearing the burdens of others. It is only natural that you sympathize. But you must relinquish the responsibility to your mate. That will be quite difficult for you if you respect your abilities to transform unpleasant outcomes more than you respect your mate's abilities. Secretly you have a small view of your mate and of God if you feel you must take the matter into your own hands.

A former client, Colette, had always found it nearly impossible not to intercede and clean up problems caused by her husband, James's, irresponsible choices. James, who was self-employed, maintained a bank account in which he set aside a requisite portion of income to pay his taxes on a quarterly basis. When the payment deadline drew near, he sheepishly informed Colette that he had "borrowed" from the tax account to buy the big-screen television that had suddenly appeared in their home the day before Super Bowl.

To cover the deficit and avoid stiff penalties and interest James wanted Colette to dip into the money she had been saving to go back to college. It was the kind of request Colette had always given in to in the past, making a convenient way for James to get off the hook—and delaying her start date at college repeatedly. James had begun to count on it.

This time Colette summoned her courage and politely refused, though her guilt feelings were nearly unbearable when James accused her of "abandoning me when I need you the most." She kept to her commitment to let James own the consequences of his choices. James did have to pay the penalties and interest for being overdue with this tax payment. It was painful, but due in large measure to Colette's refusal to give in, James has never missed his tax payments and Colette has completed her in college degree. Both of them are very proud of themselves.

If you were indifferent or unconcerned about your mate's miseries one might question your devotion. Take care, though, that you do not yield to the temptation to take ownership and responsibility of the consequences. It is theft of a valuable possession that belongs to your partner. In your mate's hands it has every potential of becoming an asset to him or her. It can only be a burdensome liability in yours. Step out of the way. Quiet your guilt and be quite suspicious of your "good intentions," before you allow them to dictate your conduct.

Love releases another to the sweetness or bitterness of the consequences of that person's choices. Arrogance only seeks the opportunity to say, "I told you so." The former edifies and enriches your mate. The latter only shames and scorns.

How well are you able to offer your mate your compassion
and concern without giving in to the urge
to solve his or her problem?

The Vow of Devout Permanence

There is nothing else that we vow to do for a lifetime except marry. It is an outrageous commitment that can only be offered by faith.

I T HAD BEEN A troublesome issue from the start of their marriage. One that they would discuss and lay to rest, only to see it rear its head again with a slightly different face upon it. This time, as usual, The Man and The Woman had eventually settled the matter, clinging to every impatient hope that it was behind them for good. They sat hand in hand, surrounded by the orchard's largest pomegranate trees. The fiery sunset seemed to celebrate their reconciliation and rekindled affections. "Will we ever finally get this right and be able to move on?" Adam wondered aloud. His question hung there, remorselessly distracting them from their previously playful mood. Each time they thought they had climbed to a new plateau in their marriage, where old conflicts could not revisit, something happened. Another obstacle to overcome, another complication to unravel, yet another lesson to be learned. "Why should we even bother trying if it doesn't get us beyond these things?" questioned Eve. Before the thought had taken full form in their minds, The Creator was there. As dusk slowly descended upon Eden, God told Adam and Eve about The Vow of Devout Permanence.

Believe me, I well understand your struggle with the idea of permanence. Only I am able to see from the beginning until the end. You will only embrace the vow of devout permanence if you are able to see your marriage and your future through the eyes of faith. Not faith in the endurance of your affections for each other, nor faith in each other's trustworthiness, nor your own sincerity. These are all variable, full to overflowing at times, scant and depleted at others. Permanence is achieved by resting on the assurance that I am willing to work wonders through you, for you, in spite of yourselves, forever.

Perhaps the wisest bit of premarital counseling I received was from the grandfatherly minister who was one of my mentors. He had no advanced degree or clinical credentials. He had simply lived and loved for a very long time and with great success. He told me that every other secret to a long-lasting marriage was second to this one: "Go into it as if the 'how long' of it is an already settled matter: forever."

Forever is an abstract idea, nearly impossible for us to fathom. We marvel at longevity, but have few visible models of the permanent, the never-ending that is at the core of the "till death do us part" pledge. Other than parenting there is no other earthly alliance we commit to permanently except matrimony. The reality of that enormous commitment cannot be fully grasped until after we have made it. Permanence is a vow we simply make by faith.

Marriage itself is a supreme act of faith. It is a bold venture into a future you have not seen, by a path you have never traveled. But without permanence as your stated objective, what is marriage but a conditional promise to live with a good friend until it feels neither as good nor as friendly as it once did?

Several years ago Aladrian rightly confronted me about a terribly unkind remark I had made to her when I mistakenly believed she had committed me to counseling a distressed friend of hers without first asking me. When my outrage about it met up with hers, we went for each other's jugulars. The results were ugly.

After voicing our indignation to no avail, we both withdrew, hurt and angry, to separate rooms. We had had heated exchanges before, but they had never felt like this one. I honestly didn't know what would come next.

Within less than five minutes of our parting, with our mutual hostility still at a fever pitch, Aladrian returned and spoke in a low, steady tone: "I don't like you very much right now; but you can be sure it's going to take more than this to knock us out." With that she turned and left the room. I suspect she said it as much to fortify her own resolve as to allay my fears. In that moment, we both knew that it was, in fact, her simple but forceful declaration of permanence.

Packing up and being done with each other would have been the easier option; we firmed our grip upon the harder one. The one where you stick around, making it feel better if you can, but making it last even if you can't. The only option that refuses to let our present distresses tempt us into forfeiting what God has intended for matrimony: stick-to-itiveness.

It's obvious what gets us rattled. We are reminded daily of the dangerous pitfalls of marriage. We seldom see longevity, let alone permanence, and when we do it doesn't often look like the kind of marriage that appeals to us. But you mustn't allow what you see around you to weaken your resolve and shorten the term of your commitment to each other.

The vow of devout permanence means a commitment to press toward perfection though it will never fully be attained in this life. Still, each moment demands and receives your heartiest efforts to wait, to give selflessly, and to rebuild if need be. It is in striving to give each other your very best and expecting that the best is yet to come.

The only ones who can do this are those who have strong spirits and determination that the hidden treasures of matrimony are found on this path. Intimate companionship is undergirded along the way, and passion's well will grow deeper if you make the choice to pursue excellence a step at a time, over a very long time.

You can make this outrageous commitment without the benefit of knowing all that you may encounter along the way. Many find such a vow unreasonable, indeed suffocating. They are those who see love and commitment as a reaction to positive events and circumstances. When pleasant circumstances bring satisfaction and fulfillment, they respond with "renewed commitment." Pleasant circumstances can easily persuade us that "forever" is infinitely possible. But when disappointing occurrences and trying circumstances are present, permanence seems idealistic and unachievable.

When committing to permanence is not a completely settled matter, we toy with the idea of escape. As long as escaping is an option there will always be a seemingly justifiable number of reasons to exercise it. Those who adhere to a vow of devout permanence keep their eyes focused on the entrances, not the exits. Having already given themselves over to an eternal commitment, they always search for a way back from the brink of disaster. Since being together from now, until . . . is a settled matter, they work their way back to reconciliation, back to affection, endurance, and perseverance. They develop a fierce tenacity and the stamina of spirit to endure the troubling and temporarily dissatisfying.

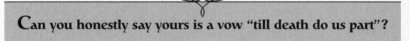

Can you honestly say yours is a vow "till death do us part"?

The Vow of Increase

The outrageous commitment to do what you may never be asked to do: to develop new abilities (or expand old ones), to attend to your spiritual and intellectual growth, and to fulfill your potential as gifts to your mate.

VE'S EARS WERE FILLED with the sound of the doves' cooing outside, as the pink light of sunrise bathed Adam's face. The heady breath of newly blossomed gardenias crept into their room as she drew in closer to the warmth radiating from her husband's slumber. After all these years she still loved to gaze at him while he slept. Soon Adam would awaken and Eve would tell him the many things she needed him to do that day. He would promise to see to them all, and tomorrow—if she was fortunate—there would be two or three fewer chores to remind him of. The Woman considered their life together. No one had ever hurt them as they had hurt each other at times. Yet, no other human being had ever given either of them as much joy as they had given each other. It was not completely logical to her, but Eve now knew that only death would ever separate them. It had taken a very long time, but The Man and The Woman had grown to realize that neither of them truly deserved the other's love, but they had it anyway. The Creator was watching them, delighting to no end that Adam and Eve had learned and were continuing to learn The Vow of Increase.

See that there is ever more of you to share with your beloved today than there was yesterday. More strength. More determination. More genuine compassion and wisdom. More humor, patience, and creativity. More of your hopes, your hurts, and your secrets. Yesterday's struggles have made you wiser. Yesterday's labors made you more prosperous. Yesterday's lack made you more appreciative of today's abundance and My abiding faithfulness. I am shaping, refining, and polishing every part of you, your character, mind, body, and spirit. Let there forever be something new and better about you to display before your mate.

There is no place in marriage for stagnation. It breeds boredom—
the archenemy of enduring marriage. Since the day you wed, is
there anything new to admire about the kind of spouse you have
become? Stagnation means your mate keeps experiencing the same
you and is seldom allowed exposure to who and what you are
becoming. Notice how there is nothing good that you have learned,
received, or experienced that cannot directly benefit your mate in
some way.

Doyle and Evelyn came for counseling, having toyed with the idea
of ending their marriage after more than sixteen years. Unlike the
couples who typically seek my services, they insisted that they were
not angry with each other and had no complaints of infidelity, broken
promises, or festering resentments. They simply had become profoundly bored with each other.

Evelyn and Doyle dryly characterized each other with adjectives
like *dependable, consistent,* and *steady.* When I asked them to
describe the most admirable and endearing qualities they had seen
their mate gain since marriage, neither of them could. Each saw the
other as exactly the same—no worse, but certainly no better—as
when they first said "I do." Sadly, they had spent sixteen years *maintaining* but not *improving* upon themselves in any measurable way.

One hugely important but often overlooked commitment in marriage is to deliberately and aggressively pursue self-improvement: to
develop new talents, or expand old ones, to increase spiritually and
intellectually, to upgrade your expertise, your communication skills,
and your practical wisdom. The kind of growing attraction needed to
keep your relationship progressing to new levels of mutual interest
and passion requires new and improved qualities that are visible to
your mate to admire and appreciate. It can become quite easy for the

two of you to keep offering your mate nothing but the old and reliable, rather than the new and improved.

Friends, colleagues, and perfect strangers will often have a clearer view of the changes in you, while the one to whom you have promised *forever* sees only who you were the day you made the promise.

How are you demonstrating daily that you are maturing in the disciplines of marriage? How are you sharing the fruit of that growth with your mate? Is it showing up by your increased levels of selflessness or discipline or ingenuity? Are you now able to speak with increased honesty and to listen with heightened sensitivity?

Remember, your marriage vow was to love, honor, and cherish with the same stalwart commitment forever. It was by no means a promise to remain the same person that you were forever. For either of you to expect that is either arrogance or resignation. Neither of you is a finished product. You are both works-in-progress.

Your ongoing commitment to personal growth and development is one powerful antidote to stagnation in your marriage. Your union increases in depth and value as you mature, continually showing signs that you have earnestly tried to polish yourself and that your efforts are working.

If you have no new life-changing experiences to share, no new ideas, insights, accomplishments, or dreams, no new faith, talents, laughter, or sorrows that you are willing to offer your mate access to, you are a book ended after the first chapter.

With every fearful hesitation cast aside, will you proudly unveil, for your beloved, the real you? Please do, because, at this moment, you are more and know more and have more of yourself to offer than ever before.

Since this time last year, what about you is measurably
"new and improved" and noticed approvingly by your mate?

The Vow of Shared Bliss

The outrageous commitment to freely disclose your private joys and triumphs to your mate in spite of the effort, in spite of the risks.

THEY TALKED WELL INTO the night, both of them venting their feelings, fears, contemplating aloud their complaints, frustrations, and disappointments by turn. They had always considered this ability to speak so freely of their burdens to be a strength of their union. Together, bathed in each other's melancholy, they had fallen asleep. When they awakened, The Creator invited The First Couple to the southern meadows, arguably the most beautiful place in Eden. The Man and The Woman had had many memorable days of carefree enjoyment here among the vibrant flowering shrubs and the intoxicating fragrances of jasmine and lavender. This visit was no different. But after an hour there, The First Couple found themselves struggling to make conversation with each other. "You're so quiet," God observed. "We spoke of all that concerns us last night. There is nothing left for us to resolve," offered Adam. "It is all so perfectly wonderful here we find it difficult to contain our delight," added Eve. "Then why must you contain it at all? Speak of your delight," encouraged The Creator as He stood in the shadow of a budding wisteria tree and shared with Adam and Eve The Vow of Shared Bliss.

I don't even try to contain My joy in loving you. I not only want you to know what delights Me, but that you find My joy contagious. It is a radical choice to give where you can't be assured of what you will be given back. But the bond of the spirit that is marriage cannot thrive if the joyfulness of your spirit is kept to yourself. It is an act of generosity to share your bliss with each other, and an act of bravery to welcome your beloved into it with you.

I was booked for a speaking engagement on the idyllic island of Bermuda. Aladrian came along, both of us hoping to squeeze in a romantic minivacation after my work was done. It was a long flight. I was already exhausted from several caffeine-charged nights editing a book that was approaching its deadline. Sleep-deprived and cranky, I spent much of the more than six-hour flight griping about my workload to a joyfully paradise-bound Aladrian. For the first couple of hours she listened attentively, but soon she discovered that her attempts to change the subject to the wonderful vacation before us were met with more of my complaints and self-pity. My wife then plugged in her CD headphones and tuned me out for the rest of the flight.

My mood changed completely when we entered our hotel room and I spotted the large terrace affording us a drop-dead view of the Atlantic Ocean. I sat for over an hour taking it all in. Though I was completely silent, my delight was apparent to Aladrian. I was clearly in my bliss. She finally approached me to say, "I'd love it if you were as willing to tell me about how good this feels to you as you were to tell me how awful you were feeling on the plane."

Sometimes married folk take the idea of "unspeakable joy" too far. You were never meant to burden each other with all your sorrows but hoard your joys to yourself. There is only the thinnest veneer of intimacy between you if your joys and triumphs are routinely treated as top secrets. Never allow only your burdens and concerns, your disappointments and complaints, to be your only place of fellowship. The one who walks beside you in darkness must always be invited to celebrate with you when midnight turns to daylight.

Inviting your mate to share your joy is one of the purely selfless and most generous acts of matrimony. If your mate is accustomed only to the sights and sounds of your discontent—your disapproving frown, your depressed mood, or your defeated expressions—you are extending a daily invitation for your beloved to join you in your gloom. It's a sure way to make the idea of sharing life with you forever quite unappealing. You become exhibit A of all that's wrong with marriage.

Why then is there such a temptation to broadcast your sorrows and complaints but to keep your joys from your mate's view? Sharing anything involves risk, either that the thing shared will be taken away, or that it will be mishandled. That's why it's often much easier to share what has made you sorrowful than what has brought you joy.

Joy is not something you want to be relieved of. In fact, you find so little of it that your possession of it feels precarious at best, and sharing it exposes it to the sometimes clumsy but very human responses of your mate. When you encounter disinterest or worse, rather than enthusiasm, you can be prompted to push your joy back to the safe place of your own heart. You miss so much when you and your beloved do not have fellowship around the glorious events and circumstances of your lives.

How much does your spouse know about the things in your life that give you the greatest joy and satisfaction at this very moment? It takes only a fleeting glance at you to detect your sorrow. It takes a clear invitation and explanation for your mate to know the source and the magnitude of your joyfulness. You alone possess the key to this treasure and others. Placing your joy in the care of your mate reveals that you trust your beloved with a very precious thing and extends to him or her an invitation to bring into your life more of what makes you blissful. Keeping your joy to and for yourself for fear that your partner will dampen it is to keep it from knowing its fulfillment.

If long ago you adopted a role in the marriage that makes joyful adulation, excitement, and noticeable happiness out of character, you'll have no use for expressing your joy. If you have cast yourself in the role of The Put Upon, The Weary, The Responsible Endurer, or The Serious Contemplator, you will work hard not to do damage to your image or allow the appearance of anything inconsistent with it.

Sheer bliss and the excitement of good news are out of character with these roles. Does your beloved know your sad stories, but not your good news?

It is not your sorrow that most threatens to distance you from each other. It is your joy, kept hushed and safely hidden, a secret never told to the one you love, but smuggled away to be shared only with those whom you are sure will rejoice the way you want them to.

The one you married will grow in the ability to celebrate with you by being given the opportunity repeatedly. You will grow in your ability to accept and appreciate your partner's way of honoring your joy as you keep offering your good news; and though your mate's celebration style is not your own, you will be increasingly able to discern his or her enthusiasm.

By spending time around you does your spouse
learn more about what is burdening you or
what is delighting you? And why?

The Vow of Reflection

A shaky self-image may not allow your mate to fully grasp all that impresses you about him or her without being repeatedly reminded by you—the one who is already thoroughly convinced that it is true.

THE WOMAN WAS ON hands and knees harvesting mushrooms when she felt her husband's eyes trained on her. Eve was about to ask him what was wrong when he swept her up in his arms and kissed her passionately. She was startled. "Wife, have you any idea what an incredible woman you are?" Eve laughed. "If this is how you return after a day of hard work, I shall send you out tomorrow with much more to do!" she said, attempting to free herself and return to her foraging. Adam held her in his embrace. "I watched you today. I hid myself and watched as you moved about, tending to your herbs, preparing the barley cakes, and making our children scream with laughter. I realized how much you do for us and how well you do it. You, my darling, are more than wonderful. Sometimes I cannot believe that you are really mine!" The Man went on. "You only say that because you have no one else to compare me to," Eve interjected, embarrassed by her husband's adoration. She fidgeted awkwardly in his arms and tried unsuccessfully to change the subject. The Woman wished it were not so, but her husband's words and his enthusiasm made her uncomfortable and not a little suspicious. The warm evening breeze swirled about them as He appeared. With a gentle touch beneath her chin, God lifted Eve's face to meet His gaze. Then He explained The Vow of Reflection.

You can be so hard on yourselves. It is I who work in your conscience, pointing out a flaw in your character or conduct that must be set aright. You readily agree and often go on to make the fault sound more heinous than it is. But when I speak in glowing terms of how much I love you and why I do, you barely hear My words and struggle to believe them. I see your discomfort. I feel your pain as you struggle to accept the free fall of My affection. But I am completely undeterred in My efforts

toward you. I have every intention of making you know how profoundly I love you and how much more I want to make you into. And that is exactly what I want you to do for each other. It is a mortal's reflection of the kind of positive "finger-pointing" I do. I whisper, repeatedly, the sometimes hard-to-believe truth of who you are and how much you mean to Me, until you begin to live as if what I see in you is the absolute truth.

When you reflect the good in another person it is often much harder for him or her to accept than you might imagine. Some of us are more prepared to hear what's wrong with us than what's right. In any marriage there is typically at least one partner who is still too hard at work looking beyond his or her imperfections to see what the mate finds completely irresistible. At times she wonders why you want her. How can you find her so desirable?

Self-doubt, lack of self-confidence, distorted self-images, or persuasively painful experiences from his or her past can make it quite difficult for your mate to believe the gloriously positive pronouncements you make. He struggles to see what you see and can't help thinking you are up to something. Yet it is vital that you declare what you see and what you sincerely believe anyway. In spite of your mate's uneasiness and in spite of the fact that he or she is unlikely to believe you anytime soon. Your mate may not be able to grasp the truth without being reminded of it repeatedly by someone who is already convinced of it.

Lisa and Ahmad came in for counseling after being married nine months. Lisa had become perplexed and annoyed by Ahmad's constantly "begging for criticism." Though she deeply loved him and considered him to be her perfect soul mate, she had grown tired of his resistance to every positive comment she made about him. Ahmad actually sought Lisa's criticism so that he could improve himself as a man and a husband. Right in my office, I saw him become tense and agitated as Lisa described to me Ahmad's many exemplary attributes that had first attracted her to him. "Stop!" he cried out, as if in pain. "How can you see these things in me?"

Lisa had tired of trying to convince him. She wanted Ahmad to accept and appreciate her admiration. Since he couldn't or wouldn't, she stopped offering it. I pointed out that for her to silence her praise would only help validate Ahmad's distorted opinion of himself. Her job was to keep singing his praises until they became a familiar echoing drone that he could choose to believe or reject. If someone close keeps singing the same song, eventually you are likely to learn it and catch yourself singing it on your own.

When you speak of life and dare your spouse to believe beauty he cannot see, giftedness he doubts, strength he can't feel, and innate value he cannot imagine that he possesses, you challenge him to believe and recognize what you have found wonderfully true. Though your efforts alone will never be enough to vanquish your mate's self-doubts, you will offer a constant, compelling reminder of truth that he or she finds hard to believe.

Each time you do you'll give your mate a fresh opportunity to catch an impressive reflection in your admiring eyes, and in your persistent words. Hopefully the day will come when your mate will choose to believe what you believe, not merely because you said it over and over again, but because it's been absolutely true about him or her all along.

In what specific ways do you keep confronting your mate with the glorious truth about himself or herself?

The Vow of Self-Enhancement

If you want to be found desirable and attractive to your mate you must make the outrageous commitment to adjust your personal style toward your mate's tastes and preferences— not just your own.

ADAM HAD NOT MEANT TO hurt her feelings, but he knew he had. "Why don't you ever decorate your hair with flowers anymore?" he had asked. It had been quite some time since she had woven strands of freesia into her long locks. Whenever she did so the sight of her flowing mane always made Adam want to draw her close and lose himself in her sweet fragrance. "Are you trying to say there's something wrong with how I look now?" Eve asked with annoyance. "Must I always ornament myself before you'll find me attractive enough?" She knelt to appraise herself in the reflection pool. Adam, seeing her troubled expression, struggled to make himself clear. "There is nothing wrong with how you look. You just used to do more with your hair and, well, I liked it, that's all." Eve kicked a pebble into the pool, blurring her pouting image. When the water settled, another image was visible there. It was not Adam. The Creator was standing just behind Eve and began to speak to them both about The Vow of Self-Enhancement.

You are the signature expression of My artistry and creativity. I spoke worlds into existence out of nothing. Self-improvement is not creating out of nothing, but a far simpler task. It is simply that you enrich and enhance to the fullest what I have already created. I have well equipped you to enhance the beauty and value of all that I have given you and all that you are. By choosing to enhance and maintain yourself in ways that are attractive to your mate, you powerfully influence his or her desire and delight in you.

Neither of us ever held to the notion that once married we gave up the right to govern our style and appearance according to our own personal tastes. We prided ourselves on how we granted each other the freedom to present ourselves as we each desired. When one of us stood before the mirror to make a final decision, whether about hairstyle or shoe color, we'd often inquire of the other, "Which do you like best?" The answer was always the same: "It's totally up to you. You'll look great to me either way." At first we sincerely meant it, too. That is until Aladrian suddenly developed a burning desire for a severely short new hairdo and for the dramatically square-toed pumps that had become the latest rage in women's shoes. This all occurred at about the same time that I had taken to sporting a thin, shadowy beard and a small gold earring.

Though both of us thought our own new look stunning, we found each other to have undergone a sudden and alarming drop in attractiveness. Her new hairstyle made me think "military" and the shoes, from a distance, made it seem to me that my wife was walking about in giant leather boxes. To Aladrian my fashionable new stubble made me look as if my face badly needed scrubbing and that my earring brought unappealing images of Mr. Clean to mind. After several weeks of winning rave reviews from friends and enemies alike, we realized that being gorgeously appealing to each other mattered far more to us than we had ever thought—and that we had the power to make it happen *if* we were willing to bend our look toward our mate's preferences, not just our own.

Love is essentially an internal commitment of one's will, a deliberate decision that is then demonstrated by acts of caring self-sacrifice. So while to love or not to love is a monumental choice, anyone with a will can make that choice at any given moment. The decision to love may be influenced by external factors but it is not derived from them. That's why love thrives no matter what the object of that love does or does not do, no matter the person's attractiveness, intelligence, charm, or the lack of it. Love is bestowed upon whom you decide to give it to. Thus you should rightly expect your spouse to have made the choice to love you just as you are. However, you should not assume that your mate's finding you attractive and desirable works the same way.

Just as surely as to love is a decision from within the giver of it, *attraction* is stimulated externally by the traits, qualities, characteristics, and appearance of the object of that desire. Our trouble is not that we expect our mates to love us as we are, but that we expect them to unwaveringly like us the way we choose to look as well. *Attraction* is an emotional response to a multitude of attributes, many of which are visual ones. Love is a willful decision and is to be offered unconditionally. Attraction is conditional. It is determined by the degree to which one meets the unique personal tastes and preferences of the beholder.

Though the willful commitment to love is a more profound thing than attraction and likability, attraction and likability are of no small significance. One who wants to be desired and appreciated by her or his spouse must influence that to happen by developing and enhancing herself or himself to the highest possible levels. Though never aiming to change *who* we are, we all are challenged to keep working to change *how* we are into a more wonderfully appealing creation who, to the fullest extent, can stimulate our spouse's attraction to us.

Pursuing consistent self-enhancement is a vital commitment— and one whose importance is often underestimated or altogether ignored. It is not a demand made of you; it is an opportunity available to you. I shudder at the sight of husbands and wives who no longer hold any attraction and desire for each other and yet are not willing to work to stimulate it again. Taking each other's tastes and preferences for granted are the pitfalls of familiarity.

Pay close attention to the positive comments your spouse makes about your appearance. They reveal the elements of your appearance that most appeal to the one you love. Adjust your look to emphasize them. Also note your mate's negative comments about others' appearance. They offer clues as to what they find unattractive and they indicate an opportunity to make changes that appeal to both of you when possible, but especially to your mate.

We want to see approval and adoration in each other's eyes. We want to be the object of each other's unbridled passion. We all want these same treasures from each other. You may influence that by making self-enhancement, with the input of your mate, your lifelong commitment.

How have you come to know your mate's tastes and preferences, by asking or by making assumptions?

The Vow of Decisiveness

To finally commit to one of your options is to be willing to let go of the dozens of others you could have chosen.

THE ONLY THING THEY completely agreed upon was the need for more living space. Relocating was an option, but that involved building again. Eve had suggested that they simply enlarge their current shelter, but Adam was concerned about sacrificing the space around their home that was needed for gardening and such. They had had countless conversations about the advantages and disadvantages of each choice. He continued to lean toward building a new dwelling elsewhere, while she favored adding on to their present one. Each of them hoped the other would make the final decision. Months passed as they waited, all the while complaining about how crowded they were, but fearful of making the "wrong" choice. One evening, during yet another eternally inconclusive discussion, The Creator entered the room and placed Himself squarely between them. *"Decide something!"* was at first all He said. They were momentarily startled by His presence, and even more so by the firmness of His tone. Then, having gained their full attention, God began to explain The Vow of Decisiveness.

I have established the universe in such a way that some things that need to happen will not unless you, out of all your endless options, finally make a choice and commit yourselves to it. If you procrastinate, never settling on a course of action, or vacillate between two possibilities, you may later find it difficult, if not impossible, to catch up with great blessings I had prepared for you, whichever option you had picked. As much as I want you to use wisdom in your deciding, I want you to exercise courage and granite-solid faith as well. You may be certain that it is not your ingenuity and infallible judgment that keep you afloat. I alone do

*that. Whichever choice you make, I am there, on the other side of it,
more than able to cause it all to work together for good.*

Making a commitment of any sort means narrowing your options.
It means sacrificing the comfort of having a full menu of choices
and an unlimited amount of time to pick one. In marriage it means
the two of you will eventually force yourselves to cease the discussion of an issue's pros and cons and move to decide exactly what you
are going to do. Of course the outrageous part is that you'll have to be
ready—for better or for worse—to live with the consequences of your
decision.

Each possible option has its own set of consequences attached to
it. If you choose to live in the city you could lose the peace and quiet
of the suburbs; if you live in the suburbs you will forgo the stimulat-
ing bustle of the city. If you choose to spend your unexpected wind-
fall now you can't save it for later. Save it for the future and you won't
be able to buy something you love today.

It is our dread of the consequences that keeps us incessantly
mulling things over. Or we become especially timid to make big decisions because in marriage someone else's life is involved. Making
choices about your life together—careers, children, money, responsibilities, when to commend, confront, or console each other—will be
necessary each day. Procrastination only causes you to carry over into
tomorrow what could have been settled today. Narrowing our options
in favor of a specific choice should not be hastily done, but sooner
rather than later, it must be done, and definitely. When you exercise
any option, you must be ready to boldly release the dozens of others
you could have chosen. Otherwise the two of you will endlessly circle
around hard choices, afraid to give a solid "yes" to any one of them,

and fearful of saying "no" to the rest of them. Our dread of ending up with anything less than perfection easily gets the best of us.

Timidity and hesitation are sure to cost you far more than they benefit you. From the beginning of your marriage what you envisioned was a true partnership in every sense of the word. Make every effort to eagerly pursue wise counsel from others, but keep the responsibility of final decision making to yourselves.

Married life keeps proving that when my wife and I have made a decision that didn't turn out as we hoped, cleaning up or living with the consequences is almost never as difficult as enduring the problems that arise from indecisiveness and delay. In taking the risk to make decisions together in a timely fashion, you will experience a growing capacity for intimate collaboration and interdependence. You will begin to reap the harvest of your "perfect" choices or you will work together to redeem the consequences of your "bad" ones.

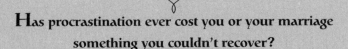

Has procrastination ever cost you or your marriage
something you couldn't recover?

The Vow of Dethronement

When you began to measure your spouse's love and commitment according to how much, or how little, he or she reduced your insecurities, you handed over your own possessions and made them his or her burden. It is only right for you to bear it, but oppressive for your mate to have to do so.

EVE SAT ON A ROCK and watched as a school of minnows rhythmically made its way through the clear, chilly water. She had left Adam playing with their sons. She was certain none of them noticed her leaving, much less how sad she had been. The Woman sensed that The Creator was near but wanted no one—not even Him—to question her melancholy. After some time He approached her. "There you are, Eve!" "Yes, here I am, alone and forgotten. And, as always, no one at my home would know or care," Eve lamented. "Is that so?" The Marriage Maker inquired, in a way that urged more detail. The floodgates opened and Eve told Him exactly what was on her mind. "Neither Adam nor our sons have any idea of how much I have had to give up to serve them. I deserve more understanding and appreciation from them. Perhaps if I stay away for a while their gratitude will increase." God eyed her sympathetically, then laughed out loud and drew her close. "Oh, daughter," He said, the warmth of His hug lessening the sting of His amusement with her, "you cannot make anyone do anything. You'll only weary yourself trying." Then He explained The Vow of Dethronement.

Your marriage has no room for any other exalted one but Me. I alone reign over all that pertains to you. There is no need for two of us to sit on the throne of your life. I have plans for your pain. I have a firm grip on your most stubborn but fragile insecurities, and your most intimidating anxieties—the things you don't want to talk about, don't want to face, don't want to feel. The things you are determined you'll never let happen again. At times I do turn up the intensity of them, or allow them to continue, but not to torment you. It is to increase your resilience and courage, and to build in you the faith that comes from having no one

*else to rely upon but Me. You are certain to be confronted with feelings
you don't want to feel and insecurities you don't want to acknowledge,
self-centeredness you don't want to own. Let me show you how to live
with a deep desire for your mate's love and care, but no longer a desperate need of it. Come down from the throne. Only then will you discover
that there is so much more love and satisfaction available to you.*

When one of you is the king (or queen) of the hill the other must
dutifully bow before your sensitivities and insecurities. Self-
aggrandizement always isolates you from the one you love. We
enthrone ourselves when we act as if our struggles and sorrows are
unique and that we are due special accommodation because of them.
This pretense of "uniqueness" is trouble from the very start. It will
lead you to view yourself in such a self-exalted way that no one will
ever be able to love you in a way that you'd ever consider good
enough. You'll become a martyr in your own eyes.

Marriage is no place for martyrs. Martyrs are completely unaware
that their false sense of humility and self-sacrifice mask a secret
desire for those who love them to prove it by bowing down to them.

We run the risk of portraying ourselves as so extraordinarily vulnerable, our burdens so heavy, our feelings so fragile, that no one
could possibly appreciate what we must be going through. The self-
enthroned want an unlimited number of matrimonial "get-out-of-jail-
free" cards on account of All That I Have Been Through or
Everything I Have to Deal With.

But "The "Special One" is certain to become "The Lonely One,"
because you cannot live upon a mountain—where the standards of
excellence are more rigorous, demands and responsibilities more
stringent, and needs so unusually complex—and live richly and intimately with each other in marriage's day in and day out.

This is not a matter of egotistical conceit at work. The fear of inadequacy craves an "extraordinary" reaction to compensate for it. Fear of being seen as undesirable requires "special" challenges to explain away the sense of inevitable rejection. It is a well-plotted strategy born from fear: self-protection by self-exaltation. Self-enthronement keeps you from working to master these sensitivities, rather than being mastered by them.

Requiring your mate to be just as you want him or her to be means restricting his or her freedom, making your partner conform to your fears or sensitivities, and your idea of what's appropriately caring conduct. Love encourages growth in individuality. It is self-centeredness that demands that a spouse not do that, say that, or choose that, simply because it doesn't feel good to you. It falsely justifies your resentment of the mate who failed to meet your towering requirements for tending to your fears, or jealousies, or angers, or possessiveness, or bitterness.

There will always be times when the uniquely challenging events and responsibilities of your life will confront you and thrust you into the necessity of your own solitary exertions. This is simply an indication that our individual lives are full of extraordinary circumstances and special burdens that require us to deal, at times, with what others don't have to. But these are the experiences that are meant to refine you, not define you. Your feelings and your needs are not nearly as unusual as you once thought. You will no longer need to suffer the loneliness, frustration, and resentment that eventually consume The Special One.

Embracing the Vow of Dethronement is to label yourself as marvelously ordinary, a member of that hapless club of runs of the mill, comprised of "everybody else," including the one you married. Surrendering your crown means you will become one *of* us, no longer one *over* and *above* us. There, you will find a level of genuinely intimate companionship that can only exist between equals who stand side by side.

In what sense have you felt the need to maintain the upper hand in your marriage?

The Vow of Silence

The outrageous commitment to listen and observe intently and undefensively, giving thorough contemplation to what your mate has said or done before (or instead of) rushing to respond.

I T HAD BEEN AN excruciatingly long visit with the couple from the foothills, and Adam was not sorry to see them go. "She did nothing but complain from the moment they arrived." Adam huffed as he shut the door behind their parting guests. "'He never carries anything for me. He always expects his wishes to be considered, but not mine.'" Adam mimicked the woman's annoying whine. Eve, who was at first lost in her thoughts, now spoke. "With all her railings about him, he never seems to change in any way." She too had found the woman's outbursts unsettling; yet she could well relate to her complaints. "If he is that horrible, why does she stay with him?" Adam wondered aloud, completely oblivious to Eve's struggle to lift a heavy water pot to the hearth. Annoyed, Eve was just about to take this opportunity to chide Adam for the very same inattentiveness as the woman's husband had shown. But when she tried to speak her words would not come out. The next words spoken were neither hers nor Adam's, but those of The Creator, who had come to teach them The Vow of Silence.

It is not necessary to comment upon everything. Perhaps the fact that, by My words, I spoke the entire universe into existence makes you think that anything significant must be voiced. At times no response is the perfect response. Silence allows Me the opportunity to arrange and rearrange your perceptions and your motives before you announce them. This cannot happen if you are in such haste to chide each other and to declare your every displeasure, drowning out My still, small voice inside you. Silence can be your most timely and eloquent response.

It is so hard for us to trust the silence. A gentle response is hard enough. No response feels absolutely criminal. We feel there need always be an assertive, well-articulated position statement made to our mates about nearly everything—especially at the first signs of a slight or an offense.

At times what may appear to be bold self-expression is no more than an anxious attempt to gain the upper hand, save face, or show off our clever wit. Silence would seem to put us at risk of losing out on something we fear we *must* have: attention. Choosing not to answer back, to take issue, to vilify your mate's behavior or justify your own, means you could appear wrong, or weak—or both. Your choice of well-timed silence is the greatest proof of your incredible fortitude. Only the confident and self-contained can pull this off successfully.

Ours is such a noisy existence. The constant din of endless chatter is all around us. There is no such thing as achieving any kind of bond of intimacy without putting your thoughts, feelings, and commitments into words. The skillful use of silence is as vital to your marriage as oxygen is to life. When you or your mate's every passing remark, meaningless expression, or spontaneous gesture must be analyzed and commented upon, too much attention is being paid to what does not deserve it. Ultimately it proves to be a great distraction that leaves husbands and wives searching for words instead of understanding and moving toward action.

When I speak of silence, I am not referring to the cruel withdrawal that occurs when, out of selfishness, apathy, or anger one or both of you have no more desire to reveal your thoughts and feelings to each other. That is not constructive silence; it is a harmful expression of disinterest. The silence that enriches is a commitment to listen intently and then give thorough consideration to what your mate has said or done before—(and perhaps instead of)—rushing to confront it with a barrage of words.

To your mate, the gift of your well-chosen silence can mean the difference between feeling tolerated and being truly cared for. Your silence in conversation can be an acknowledgment that what he or she has to say matters enough to you to hear it fully. Silence opens the door to reason and reflection, the essentials of a helpful response.

Your verbal restraint when you are in conflict is one of the beneficial skills you bring to each other in marriage. You must not allow your only communication to be by speaking. Sometimes it is wise to resist the intense desire to set each other straight. Your choice of words (and your timing in using them) has the power to strengthen your bond of intimacy and mutual appreciation or to destroy it. Keep focused on your objective and what will serve it best—silence or words.

Your replies should not be motivated by the desire to be right, but the desire to gain understanding, edify your mate, and elevate your marriage. To successfully achieve these objectives you'll do well to keep your initial thoughts to yourself, seeking to hear instead of rushing to be heard.

How often does your spouse say or do something you find annoying and you immediately voice your disapproval, then instantly regret it because the issue simply wasn't worthy of comment?

The Vow of Uncertainty

Whatever we are convinced will never change is what we are most in danger of taking for granted.

I HEAR THEY NO LONGER sleep together and she refuses to even consider reconciliation. Can you imagine that?" said Eve. Adam responded with a grimace, disbelief evident in his voice, "No, I cannot even imagine it. Anyway, I'm sure that could never happen to us. I'd never allow myself to become that stubborn," said The Man. "And I'm not so frail that I would ever let you treat me as he treats her," Eve continued. "And even with all our difficulties, we could never consider giving up." They were suddenly quiet, struck dumb by the folly of their words. There had been times when walking out seemed to them the only wise choice. Times when their fits of anger were so intense that they suspected it to be what hatred must feel like. Suddenly they felt far less assured than they had just seconds before. "Be careful of what you think you know about your future," The Creator gently warned. With that He began to teach them The Vow of Uncertainty.

You can be certain of nothing except who I am, what I say, and how deeply I love you. All else remains to be seen. Merely wishing to be completely assured isn't enough to make it so. Be only certain of this: I know every twist and turn, all that is here today and gone tomorrow, every hidden weakness and secret strength of your union. Only the one responsible for navigating your life needs to be certain of everything that may come up. Today I encourage the two of you to willingly enter the fellowship of uncertainty. It is a faith-filled, aggressive dependence on Me and My firm grip on tomorrow. You can comfortably accept the fact that you are completely uncertain of what bliss or difficulty may come, but certain that in all earnestness you are truly with and for your mate, and that I am with and for you both.

If, in marriage, you feel certain that your every loving act will be reciprocated and that your every hope will be fulfilled, you've set yourself up for a great deal of disappointment. Certainty is the haughty insistence that your future together must live up to all your dreams. Whatever you are convinced is unchangeable is what you are in danger of taking for granted.

One of the cardinal rules of good marriage counseling is that the therapist should never rush to try and convince troubled clients that "everything is going to turn out just fine." In fact, the distress of being uncertain of how (or if) the relationship will ever get back on track is, at the start, a couple's greatest asset. Spouses in crisis who seek help from me are usually powerfully motivated by their uncertainty about the future. Not knowing what might happen with their marriage either emboldens them—or frightens them—enough to do work on themselves and the marriage that they would not even have considered doing before.

Those who are certain of eternal commitment will see no need of recommitting each day. Those who are certain they have once and for all declared their love and affection (and have borne witness to its being returned to them) see no need to continue declaring it. And husbands and wives who are certain this or that crisis could never happen to them will never consider the need to guard themselves against it. Beware of the kind of "certainty" that is really only naïve presumption.

Aladrian and I were certain it all had to be a big mistake when a routine insurance examination indicated that I had a virtually undetectable but life-threatening heart defect. Our life together took a sudden turn away from what we had unquestioningly considered "certain": that our athletic good health would go on forever. That we'd work hard, then retire to enjoy many more years of getting to know the world and each other better than ever. And finally, that our prayers would be answered and we would quietly pass away in each other's arms, both with the look of supreme contentment upon our faces.

Now they were telling me that my future, and all that I was always certain it had to include, hung in a fragile state of uncertainty. I retreated to my own silent world of brooding and self-pity. After several days, when it came to my marriage, I almost gave my permission to not give a damn. Neither I nor Aladrian could find our familiar rudder of certainty to navigate our words, our goals, or our choices.

I never said it, but I was angry that I had to become for my wife and for myself the kind of husband who could continue to love, honor, and cherish without the encouraging assurances of what tomorrow would look like—or whether there would even be one.

Happily my diagnosis was later found to have been accurate, but it was in this gray fog-laden detour on our shared journey toward a satisfyingly certain future that my wife and I rediscovered each other. We learned that limping along with each other's faithful companionship on a detour was undeniably more profound than mindlessly pushing ahead toward the naïve, unwaveringly happy fantasy, that marriage we had designed to include no life-threatening surprises.

If you consider yourself a practical person, not given to foolish speculation or wishful thinking, upon close examination you may discover that you do maintain an internal list of what you consider confirmed about your mate, yourself, and your marriage. And once you label anything as such, you will live your life accordingly. Those who are devoted to their certainties will see only that which agrees with them. All else will be completely overlooked or "spun" in such a way that it does not challenge what you are certain of, but only confirms it.

If, deep down, you think the two of you are solely responsible for the preservation of your marriage, you may be inclined to insist that your mate constantly demonstrate in word and deed that your certainties are well founded. What an impossible chore it becomes to have to keep convincing each other that there is nothing of which you need ever be uncertain. Yet, giving up your certainties will leave you with what you most despise: unanswered questions about the future. *Will we ever have the big house on the hill? Will our children end up making us feel proud or guilty? Will we ever resolve the one issue that we've never been able to resolve? Will we grow old together without knowing infidelity or poverty or terminal illness or terminal regret?*

Therefore you needn't draw hard and fast conclusions today about any detail of your marriage. Recall the hopes you once held to before you became certain that they would never be realized. That may well be your pessimism masquerading as pragmatism. Consider all the intensely exhilarating feelings and appealing circumstances you've experienced in your marriage so consistently that it seems as though they'll continue forever without you having to work for them. That's a false sense of security masquerading as certainty.

That is why the willingness to endure uncertainty is such an essential vow of marriage. It will leave you certain of only one thing—that there is no earthly thing that you can be absolutely certain of. Your confidence and your ability to rise up to each new day, hoping for the best but willing to accept life on life's terms, will be based on the absolute faithfulness of God in the midst of life's unpredictable circumstances. Will you abandon yourself to the care of The One whose personalized displays of unlimited love repeatedly confirm that His grace really is sufficient for you? It matters not what tomorrow will bring—or even that there will be a tomorrow. Only the God who caused you to survive and flourish today is willing and able to do it again tomorrow.

Will you invest yourself fully in the marriage you have today, with no iron-clad guarantees about tomorrow?

The Vow of Compassion

The outrageous commitment to empathize by attempting to see from your mate's point of view, though it is not, and may never become, your own.

TO ADAM, HE WAS simply skipping stones by the water. To The One observing him, Adam appeared to be punishing the river. As if he envied it for being free. "She's so insecure!" The Man complained. "I cannot go off to spend any time alone without her fearing I've rejected her somehow." They had not been husband and wife very long. "She's afraid, Adam." said The Creator. "But she came from me and I have never been afraid of anything!" he shot back. "Is that so?" asked God with disbelief apparent in his tone. "Can you remember how it was before you had Eve?" Adam recalled those early, lonely days, when he was daily reminded that every living creature had a mate but him. When Eve came everything changed. Adam felt he was a part of something that was bigger than just himself. He recalled staying up nights watching her sleep, afraid he might awaken to find her gone. He *had* been afraid. It was during these moments of sobering reflection that God shared with Adam The Vow of Compassion.

Compassion is one of the least attempted but most needed virtues in any marriage. You do not struggle without My knowing it and feeling the strain along with you. You do not weep without its leaving a wet trail on My cheek. It is not only because I have omniscient understanding of your imperfections. I choose to identify with them fully as well. I want your compassion to motivate you the way it motivates My devotion to you.

At times we can be so harsh with ourselves. Our imperfections keep surfacing, reminding us that we are less virtuous than we wanted to believe we were. Our easy angers often give way to an urge to place blame and to punish ourselves. But since we cannot banish ourselves to a permanent sentence of confinement, we eventually show ourselves some grace and compassion. "After all," we tell ourselves with loads of heartfelt sympathy, "nobody's perfect." Though you may find it harder to give it, your mate needs no less of that same tender compassion that you lavish upon yourself.

Compassion is the conscious decision to place yourself directly in the path of whatever challenges your mate, to feel what he or she feels, and how it is felt. Choosing compassion is choosing to see from the other's point of view, though it is not, and may never be, your own.

You cannot afford to view your mate as so vastly different from you in his or her struggles. As long as you do, you will measure your partner's faults by a much harsher standard. And you'll feel justified in assigning labels you'd never apply to yourself, even when you exhibited the same faults. As ever-vigilant defenders of our own feelings, we can be quick to strike back when we are hurt. Where compassion is scarce, contempt and detachment are bound to seep through. A lasting marriage requires absolute consistency between how you measure imperfections—your own as well as your mate's.

My friend Gerald had always felt justified in berating his wife, Joanie, for frequently coming home from her high-power management job distracted and out of sorts. "You give them 110 percent all day and then you have nothing left for me when you get home," he'd complain.

It was only after Gerald was promoted to a challenging new position at his firm (in a department that prided itself on giving 200 percent) that he began to empathize with Joanie rather than castigate her. Now he knew firsthand what it felt like to walk in her shoes. He was no longer her accuser; empathy had brought them to a new level of partnership and mutual support. Soon thereafter Gerald and Joanie left their overly demanding jobs—to start a business and work together.

To identify with your mate's flaws has nothing to do with denying the existence of such faults or of your disappointment. Rather, it means recognizing how your partner might have done what he or she did for the same reasons that you have done your version of that same thing, or failed in your own unique way. Our faults are only different on the surface; their origins are the same—our secret fears, lusts, and self-centeredness.

Be rid of the notion that it is your mate who is the sinner and you who are the saint. Recognize that for your beloved, as for you, some progress is slow and, perhaps for a time, all but invisible. Some lofty intentions are never realized. Some character flaws are never completely shaken off. Here you are not as different as you would like to think. Might you be willing to grant the same compassion and understanding to your mate that you freely give yourself?

The greatest disservice you can do your mate is to expect a painless, perfect union and therefore declare any mistake intentional and unforgivable. In spite of your feelings to the contrary, all is not intentional and nothing is unforgivable.

Presuming our mate's innocence creates a safe place for that person to learn a different response. Compassion, mercy, and consideration are learned by example. And in marriage, the one who feels the pain of their absence must be the one to lead by example if both are to flower in the union.

How willing are you to grant the same compassion and understanding to your mate that you freely give yourself?

The Vow of Impossibility

The depth of your commitment is certain to waver when you near the perceived limits of your strength and reason; but something transformative happens in a marriage when spouses see each other—in spite of all reason—attempting what they had considered impossible.

THEY HAD NEARLY REACHED the top of the rocky cliffs where they would drink in their favorite view of Eden below. The way was arduous for Eve, who walked just ahead so Adam could keep her in sight. Then, the unthinkable happened. Adam lost his footing and slipped over the steep edge of the cliff. He had slowed himself just enough to grasp a solitary branch protruding from the rocks. Eve rushed to his aid, reaching for his free hand just at the moment that Adam's feeble branch snapped cleanly from its roots. Eve cried out to God as Adam hung desperately to her weakening grip. "You must hold on and all will be well," was all He said. "I can't!" The Man and The Woman screamed in unison. "Yes you can, and you must," urged The Creator. They could feel their hands slipping from each other's hold. Adam closed his eyes, unable to bear the hopelessness in Eve's face. It matched his own. "Let me go, Eve. Better that one of us is lost and not both." Eve knew she would be lost without him. Resolve hardened itself in her. "I won't let go! I won't." That was all He needed to hear. He touched his hand to theirs and immediately Eve's grip was strengthened tenfold, as Adam's footing locked solidly beneath him. Just moments later, as they held each other in a trembling but grateful embrace, God told Adam and Eve about The Vow of Impossibility.

Your cries that "it cannot be done" are constant in My ears. To you that sounds like pronouncements of great wisdom, but to Me only anxious chatter. You cannot perform marriage miracles without My contribution; but I often choose not to perform them without yours. It is I who walk with ease upon the waves, but if you are bold enough you can join Me.

In marriage more so than any other endeavor, we use the word "impossible" to justify our refusal to try the untried. Marriage itself is a miracle, as is the extraordinary commitment at the heart of it. Refusing to attempt anything beyond your mortal understanding or experience is the sure pathway to defeat.

We are much too quick to see our challenges as impossibilities. Without a second thought we declare, with the utmost assurance, that we cannot forgive again, cannot say what we feel, or ask for what we need. We believe it's impossible to keep our tones and attitude kind, our broken hearts receptive, our words few, our listening generous, our grace flowing freely. But by declaring the obligations of love impractical and unrealistic, we manage to excuse ourselves from any obligation to act on them. With the melodramatic pronouncement of impossibility, we deal a death blow to any obligation to try any further. Vows and commitments can be cleanly erased with no guilt when we convince ourselves that they simply cannot be done.

Be brutally honest. What have you labeled impossible because of the kind of person you married, the kind of life you live, the unique obstacles you face, your past history, failed efforts, or simply because keeping that commitment did not prove to benefit you as much as you thought it would? Perhaps you have convinced yourself that love must present you with more acceptable options, fewer burdensome obligations. The vows are choices, but when you have chosen to offer them to your mate, they became binding commitments. Some go so far as to give lip service to their commitment, but inwardly explain it away by reminding themselves that keeping it really can't be done. Then it's downgraded to an obligation you *would* keep, but not under the existing circumstances. *"There's no way; even if I wanted to, I couldn't."* We defend our paralysis by saying, "Only God can perform miracles!"

We handily convince ourselves that the heftier commitments we made cannot be kept, when what we really mean is that they can't be kept comfortably, conveniently, and without an iron-clad guarantee of success. Commitment begins to waver as it approaches your perceived limits of your human strength and reason.

When we tell ourselves there is an area of our marriage that is beyond repair, we automatically shut off our creative problem-solving faculties. No one in his right mind will strategize about how to mend the sails on a ship he believes is already sunk.

A woman in the audience of a book-signing approached to speak to me after I had summarized my book's relationship advice. She told me that she had come to the signing for the sole purpose of disputing my premise that all relationships can be difficult to maintain, but that it's almost never impossible.

She tearfully admitted that during my talk she had come to realize that for nearly five years her only thought about her marriage was that any attempt to rebuild it would be hopeless. She and her husband's frightfully poor communication patterns and their eventual indifference toward each other had convinced her that the relationship had died.

She explained that not only had she stopped trying to *do* anything about it, she had even stopped thinking creatively about what might help them to recover. She was certain her husband had come to the same conclusion she had: impossible.

Then she realized that over the course of those five years she and her mate had become wiser and more mature in every other area of their lives. They were more effective at recognizing problems and figuring out solutions to them when it came to their careers, their relationships with others, their finances, and more. They just hadn't bothered to bring their accumulated wisdom of those years to the task of reconciling their "hopeless" marriage. *"We've both become pretty smart cookies, but we've haven't used any of it to learn how to talk to each other."*

What may appear hopeless in one phase of your marriage may be completely doable at a later stage—if you don't fall in love with the word *impossible*.

Something incredible happens in a marriage where partners watch each other attempt to do that which was once considered impossible. There is an unspoken but clear message communicated between them. "You and our marriage matter enough for me to keep hoping." "You are worth better than my best effort!" Marriage was never intended to simply expose your limits, but to stretch you far beyond them, not just for your own sake but for the sake of the one you love.

What's at the top of the list of previously kept marital commitments that you now label impossible?

The Vow of Reconciliation

The outrageous commitment to simultaneously confront your mate with the truth and protect him or her from your wrath.

THE MAN AND THE WOMAN were tired of the sound of their own voices. Getting to an early end of their ferocious dispute had become the unspoken intention of both of them. Then Eve, believing she could end the conflict without losing it, leveled Adam by resurrecting a painful embarrassment from his past. Something she had sworn never to mention again. As she expected, Adam was devastated and withdrew into bitter silence. For a few moments, Eve felt the proud flush of victory. Then guilt set in. She had to find her husband. He had not gone far. She could see the gleam of tears in his eyes. When he saw her approach, Adam turned to hide himself from her view. Eve realized that in securing her victory, she had lost. At some point during the long, sleepless night, The Creator interrupted their pained silence and spoke to them concerning The Vow of Reconciliation.

Let Me clearly state what you may find hard to believe: I am not, nor have I ever been, opposed to your battles. You have concerns that are significant to both of you and differences, from mild to extreme, in your separate points of view. There will be misunderstandings, offenses, anger, embarrassments, and the need to take each other to task about something that cannot be ignored. Arguing, My kind of arguing, is to address your differences clearly and passionately, but with the fervent intention of arriving together at an agreeable conclusion. One in which you have more, never less, of the spirit of collaboration and intimacy than when you began.

That there will be conflict in your marriage is a given. How you handle your inevitable disputes is the measure of your union's stability and your commitment. Though you must give each other the freedom to say what must be said, you will also need to set clear limits on how you go about saying it. Those who fail to establish mutually agreed upon rules of order—what is and is not fair fighting—are doomed from the outset. You'll either never argue (and thus never effectively reconcile your differences) or you'll allow yourselves to use anything within your power to do battle. No matter how selfish, insensitive, or destructive it may be.

It is not simply to be heard and understood. Or to gain sympathy or assign blame. Or to keep the peace at any cost. The goal, the place you and your partner lovingly press toward, is the restoration and renewing of your commitment to one another. You always strive to end on the same side. You don't just hope. You do.

Too often, in the absence of predetermined policies and procedures, husbands and wives come away from arguments with two threatening problems: the original conflict issue, still intact and unresolved, and a new, more volatile issue of how you argued about the original issue. Your arguments should, at the end, subtract from the list of grievances between you, not add to it.

Setting limits and boundaries on acceptable and unacceptable verbal content and behavior before you are in a heated debate is crucial. During one is nearly impossible. Afterward, it is too late to matter.

High-volume ridicule, defensiveness, unfair comparisons, tantrums, twisted facts, ultimatums, bitter sarcasm, and attention-grabbing hysteria should all be considered off-limits regardless of the circumstances. Apologies and excuses after the fact are a poor substitute for setting ground rules in advance.

The commitment to reconciliation means you both have the challenging, simultaneous tasks of confronting your mate and protecting him or her from your wrath. Those who argue most effectively are fully aware that the most they can lose in an argument is the argument itself. Not their self-esteem. Not their mate's devotion. Tell your mate what works best in communicating with you, when you are hurt or angry. Do you need to be left alone for a time to regroup (Aladrian) or do you most need to get to the end of the story quickly (me). Listen, observe, and pay careful attention to what your mate reveals about how (and how not) to approach her or him when the heat is on. Be boldly specific as you identify together the dos and don'ts of fair fighting between yourselves.

At times the most beneficial reconciliation approach is to hear each other fully, then simply agree to disagree. Some of our conflicts are not worth the risks involved in trying to force unanimous agreement where it does not and need not exist.

Decide now and forever that the focus of your conflict is reconciliation. Set some ground rules *before* you are immersed in a heated dispute. Your every conflict is an opportunity to triumph over the forces that seek to separate you.

When in conflict with your mate, do you most often hinder the reconciliation process by your blaming, justifying, or pouting?

The Vow of Surrender

Choosing to withhold the last word benefits your mate (who is certain to seem not to deserve it). It is the outrageous commitment to endure the troubling feeling that you may have cost yourself a "win."

BY THE TIME HE appeared there had been several hours of dead silence. Neither The Man nor The Woman had even glanced in each other's direction. At this point, even a glimpse might be seen as a challenge. Their well-worn dispute could be reignited into a brand new battle. Who'd walk away from the rapid-fire debate with the spoils of victory this time? Who'd deliver The Last Word? At the very same moment both Adam and Eve wondered whether the other's silence meant that the matter had finally been resolved. Or, was this simply a pause to gather more evidence, more outrage, and more angry words. They had not noticed Him standing close by in the shadows and when He finally spoke they were startled. Both rushed to explain. To accuse. To defend. To pronounce the final word on the matter. Neither got very far. For it was there, in the middle of an acacia grove on a misty, cool night in Eden that The Creator called for silence, then presented to them The Vow of Surrender.

You already have all the love, respect, and understanding you will ever need. You have it from Me, even when you don't always have it from each other. I give it liberally and I don't change My mind. Surrendering your right to have the last word is an exceptional act of self-sacrifice because it involves possessing a ready weapon, an imposing fortress, an intimidating battalion of warriors, and electing not to use them because it makes you, and the one you say you love, adversaries.

Today, as in countless days past and countless days to come, one or both of you is likely to feel the "need" to have the last word. Both of you feel that you, and you alone, know exactly what *must* be said to straighten out the unresolved issue between you. Every fiber of your being—your opinionated will, your rich vocabulary, and your most persuasive arguments—are all poised and ready to bring the matter to your preferred conclusion. And as much as we all love bringing conflicts to a conclusion, we love even more when, in the end, we got the last word.

It is the word that promises to settle everything. The word that swiftly and undeniably does away with any further risk that you could be seen as stupid, or worse, taken for a pushover. Between marriage partners having the last word symbolizes personal triumph.

While we are plotting victory, we cease to be partners who hold each other's best interests over our own. Instead we become opponents fiercely determined to defeat the other. Having to have the last word is to momentarily abandon our commitment to unity and self-sacrifice in order to win a contest.

Winning holds such overwhelming appeal to us. The possibility of it causes us to lose our heads and arm-wrestle with each other over the rights to the final pronouncements. As if our mere words could assure we get the kind of tender handling and unquestioning respect we desire from our mates.

When you are insecure and obsessed with having your way, you will seek quick, decisive victories. And you will forget that you already possess all that you are fighting to claim. You then work feverishly to protect what could never be taken from you in the first place.

When we are angry, we are not simply aiming to be heard. We are demanding that our mate perceive us as a mighty force to be reckoned with. Forcing the last word is not as much to clarify our views as to maintain our position by vanquishing all opposition to it. It is not to resolve our differences as much as it is to assert our rights, or reinforce our elevated view of ourselves. Those who secretly struggle with feelings of weakness, strive to be seen as strong. How, you ask?

By turning the tables and letting the risk of being diminished become your mate's rather than your own. You accomplish it by using witty, stinging retorts, challenge-proof declarations, an authoritarian tone, or a condescending dismissal: *"This is ridiculous. I don't want to hear any more about it."* Thus the last word has been spoken, and it was yours. But when you insist on having the final word, you abruptly end the dialogue, crowning yourself victorious, leaving your mate silenced and defeated. Victors and victims never trust each other enough to build lasting intimacy together. That is, until they learn to bite their tongues.

In the interest of dousing some sparks before they unnecessarily become flames, let some of your mate's unappreciated declarations be met by your silence. Choosing to hold your tongue is your deliberate self-sacrifice for the sake of someone who may not appear to deserve it. You needn't fear the conversation has ended. The last word has yet to be spoken. You have the rest of your lives together to talk it out. Hold your tongue for now, knowing that if you stop short of a verbal counterattack you have every potential of *later* arriving at a mutually agreeable resolution rather than escalating to a full-out war. It is the often unrecognized triumph of the one who is willing, at times, to throw up the white flag of surrender.

When, in a heated exchange with your partner, you doggedly insist upon "winning," what are you working to prove (to your mate or to yourself)? Is it worth it?

The Vow of Testimony

For your own sake, and for disenchanted husbands and
wives around you, you must testify to the miracles you have
witnessed in your marriage. Otherwise, they may never
know that such miracles are possible, and you, sadly, will
forget.

I T HAD BEEN A PLEASANT day among friends for Adam and Eve. They had enjoyed visiting other couples; it was time spent sharing news, good food, and laughter. Usually, though, before the evening ended, someone or several people would seek The First Couple for advice or a solution to a problem in their marriage. When Adam and Eve's relationship was going well they feared sounding boastful. When they were doing poorly they feared discouraging the others. Tonight, they journeyed homeward discussing the idea of curtailing these evenings with their friends. "Did you enjoy your visit with the others?" The Creator asked as He appeared from behind them. "Well, yes, at first," said Adam, "but after a while it is uncomfortable to be with them." Eve agreed. "They look to us as if we had mastered marriage and could tell them how to be successful at it too. They don't understand that we struggle too. How can we teach them?" It was the kind of response The Creator had expected. "Oh, but they do not need you to teach them lessons, they need you to bear witness to what you experience—the bitter and the sweet." With these words God began to explain The Vow of Testimony.

"They" will always be watching you. They will be listening to you. And They will learn the acts and expressions of unconditional love—rightly or wrongly—from you. I have blessed you with much. Where much is given, much will be required. By your honest testimony they will come to know that I have the power to reconcile the irreconcilable, to resurrect what has died, to navigate them through the darkest valleys, and to meet the direst needs. They must see in you evidence that the utterly outrageous, seemingly impossible commitments of marriage are honor-

able, pure, and possible. They must know that if I am trusted to, I will do exceedingly and abundantly beyond what you ever imagined—with you and for you. As you tell your story to them you reinforce your own faith as well, because each time, you remember that you have done nothing that I did not give you the means and ability to do. And remembering that, your image of Me becomes more vivid and My promises to you more believable, and your commitment to your marriage more determined.

Jorge and Irma are former clients who came to me during the early, extremely rocky years of their marriage. They had dropped out of counseling as couples often do, when either their money or their patience with the process had grown thin. At the point at which they left I had little confidence that their marriage would go the distance.

Years later a beaming Jorge and Irma showed up at a seminar I presented. At a break they proudly detailed to me how after many more years of struggle (including a couple of separations) their marriage was stronger than they had ever imagined it could be.

Not quite able to mask my disbelief, I asked them what had happened. They explained that several months prior they had opened their living room for an informal Friday night gathering of other young married couples. The evenings were spent with the couples sharing their struggles, but also the ways they were finding to overcome them. None of them were therapists. None of them had it all together. But as Jorge put it, "Some kind of way the others have helped us learn from hearing about their ups and downs and they've learned from ours." Irma, Jorge, and their friends had discovered the mutually healing benefits of "testifying."

For the sake of weary husbands and disenchanted wives, mediocre marriages and fretful futures, you must testify to the miracles you have seen in your marriage. Otherwise they may never know that such miracles are possible—and you, sadly, will forget.

Yours is a richly detailed drama, full of shared dreams and aspirations as well as plans that have sadly gone awry. It is a tale of two who, at times, know each other intimately, trust each other completely and, at other times, live with the nagging sense that they could not possibly know each other very well at all. As in every drama, there is hope and frustration, stunning gains and staggering losses, tender affections giving way to growing estrangement.

At times, you have sought those who would weep with you. But how many times have your extended seasons of struggle given way to triumphant breakthroughs without so much as a whisper of joyful gratitude from you? And how many times have you seen other couples go through what you have already been through and all you offer is a silent prayer, denying them one of the most precious things God has chosen to put within your power to give them—living proof of miraculous possibilities?

Certainly we all hesitate to expose to others what is so private. Still, it is well worth it to sacrifice yourself and the comforts of your privacy to those who have become momentarily paralyzed by despair or fatigue so that they may gain hope and comfort. Encourage and strengthen them by telling your story as if it had life-saving properties. It most assuredly does.

Each time you share a chapter of your testimony that speaks of restoration, a transformation, an improbable breakthrough, you make it clear that what is available to you is absolutely available to them. Beyond that, you will be refortified as your witness reminds you from whence you have come.

How did you go from where you were in that trying area of your marriage to where you are today? Where did you begin to trust that this too shall pass? How did you remain at peace through that which once threatened to destroy you? You must not wait until the end of the story to testify. The story does not end. Speak now and never hold your peace. Honestly. Vividly. Hopefully. Whether in hushed tones of reverence or in strident shouts of warning, testify. It is a mighty weapon against the threatening forces of impatience and ingratitude. Never forget what you have been through, and that, in spite of every obstacle, you did indeed get *through* it. There are countless other couples around you who are headed toward what you have just come through. You will heighten the possibility that they come through victoriously if you will testify to them that you did.

Have you ever experienced a bona fide marriage miracle? Who in your life needs to know about it today?

The Vow of Verbalized Gratitude

The outrageous commitment to habitually express appreciation, even for your mate's doing what he or she was "supposed" to do.

THERE HAD BEEN NO argument, no offense yet to be dealt with. But there was an undeniable feeling of distance between them. No longer did they share their thoughts and daydreams, but guarded them closely like private possessions. Each continued, in earnest, seeing to individual obligations. Every day Eve faithfully baked the raisin cakes that her husband could never get enough of. Adam continued each night to build a fire big enough to chase away the chill Eve often complained of. These days their caring acts had become perfunctory, expected but unnoticed. Neither requested nor commented upon. This day Eve was busy digging a trench around her garden when Adam came home for his dinner. "I'll do that," he said, taking the shovel from her. Without a word, Eve turned to fetch The Man's dinner. Soon she returned, bearing the bountiful meal she had prepared for him. Putting down the shovel, Adam stopped to eat in silence. Eve went back to her chore. At that time the thought of expressing appreciation to each other never even crossed their minds. Before Eve could finish her trench or Adam his meal, The Creator visited to share with them The Vow of Verbalized Gratitude.

Your marriage thrives when you are consistently nourished by each other's gracious acts. Your giving and doing for each other is the natural expression of loving commitment. When your gratitude is verbalized it is made most visible to the one you love. Even I treasure your words of appreciation. I am completely enraptured by the sound of your acknowledgments that I have done what I promised, and more besides. Be assured, in this your mate is very much like Me.

Have you not noticed that subtle, dry tension between you at times? You have not always been able to trace its origins. In the end you suspect that it is only due to the burdensome demands of your day, and you wearily plod on. But that dryness between you is often due to the infrequency of verbalized gratitude. Human nature is such that when there are few "Thank you's" expressed *to* you, in time there will be few heard *from* you. Outspoken gratitude is the window to your thankful heart. Silence offers no clues to confirm that what you did was appreciated. Without it you are left unsure and undermotivated to offer your mate the same loving gesture (or others like it) in the future.

Never allow your gratitude to go unspoken. There is so much more available to you and to your marriage if you will voice your appreciation to each other for what has already been given. Verbalized gratitude is the reminder that there is an easily overlooked inventory of good things that you do for each other in the name of love.

There is little that is more meaningful to either of you than your stated expressions of appreciation. You have an inherent desire for your mate's devoted companionship and kindness inside you. To look to your beloved to consistently offer it makes you vulnerable to her or his benevolence—or lack thereof. Expressing gratitude for your partner's demonstrated commitment to showing such a generous love is an act of humility. Strangely, one that we often prefer to show, or feel, rather than verbalize. Words take time to shape and to utter. To do so means slowing down your frantic pace to consider the acts of kindness and commitment daily shown you by your beloved.

I am not suggesting that if no gratitude is expressed that the giver's act is somehow incomplete. Many lovers perform the most grandiose gesture, then expect immediate grateful acknowledgment of it. Such a self-centered parnter keeps meticulous records of the other's supposed ingratitude. Giving is not completed by acknowledgment any more than a question is completed by an answer.

You will have missed the point too, if you are hard set on the notion that thanks need not be uttered for having done what is a fundamental obligation of matrimony. Do you believe that thanks need not be uttered for a partner's having done what is a fundamental obligation of matrimony? Do you wonder about the necessity to thank each other for your faithfulness, your conscientiousness, your tender affections, strenuous exertions, or for simply coming home at night? Certainly, you argue, these are only what one is *supposed* to do, what one has vowed and is now contractually bound to perform. You are right. Marriage does make you obligated. That, however, does not mean it deserves no verbalized gratitude. It deserves it all the more because it was an obligation that was met. One that could have been ignored, or reneged upon.

Early in my career I had what I thought was my dream job, reporting directly to a man widely considered one of the greats of my profession. He was my hero and I worked hard to please him. Though he constantly pointed out areas in which I needed to improve, he almost never showed appreciation when I did a job well. "You'll get your reward in heaven. Too much thanks goes to a man's head," he warned. Though I remained in his employ for a number of years, serving someone who kept his gratitude to himself soon became more of a chore than a delight.

Sincerely stated gratitude nourishes the soul of its recipients, making constant efforts to do what has been motivated by care and commitment the preferred choice. Each time you hastily express your thanks you take the guesswork out of your mate's knowing what conveys love and devotion to you.

I am well aware that you may come to find the idea of constantly verbalizing your gratitude burdensome. It is tempting to act as if your gratitude has already been understood, and that to utter it would be an unnecessary and redundant effort. But it is that very *unnecessary*—perhaps unexpected—effort that will cause both of you to pause for the briefest moment to recognize and celebrate that one of you has chosen to make the other richer by a kindness shown.

How would your mate describe the frequency (and sincerity) of your expressions of gratitude? Why?

The Vow of Uncommon Sense

To look beyond what your mate said or did to see what she could not bring herself to say and was not quite able to do. To love him at his most unlovable, when common sense says he doesn't deserve it and that you have nothing more to offer.

"GOOD MORNING, MY LOVE. How do you feel today?" Her gracious tone did little to charm her grouchy, bedridden husband. "I'm cold," Adam barked. Eve was already approaching with another skin to cover him. "Do you plan to feed me, or must I hunt from this bed?" She left to fetch wood. Adam did not like feeling helpless. His broken leg had brought him much pain, but it did not compare with the torture of not being able to do what he pleased. The crackle of a lively fire could soon be heard from the other room. She brought him his breakfast and kissed him passionately when she set it before him. As he ate the goat cheese and apricots, Adam watched his wife head down the path toward the fields. "She is off to do my work," he groaned. "After the awful way I've treated her." He could not understand how Eve could continue to see him as worthy of such loving care. She had listened to him grouse and complain for days and had returned nothing but kindness. And that kiss! It was as big and full of unrestrained affection as those she gave him when he had done something exceptionally kind. Adam was at a loss for words. He knew without a doubt that his wife was living out The Vow of Uncommon Sense.

I've known all along that the time would come that your common sense would grow great. You have lived with each other in a world that, though it sometimes shows the unexpected and unexplained, is usually quite predictable. You find it logical to count on the sun rising each morning and the moon each night, for rain to fall from the sky. Common sense is a gift I gave you, with every hope that you'd use it. But I must caution you against viewing all things in marriage strictly within the limits of your finite common sense. For if you do you will fail to recognize what can only be seen through the eyes of the Spirit, the super-

natural laws of faith and the limitless realities of miracles. In marriage you cannot be masters of common sense only. For if you are, you will soon become slaves to it.

Strict adherence to common sense alone will cause you to make predictions of the future based solely on what happened in the past. Those who secretly predict that a loss, disappointment, or a hurtful end are inevitable feel they can salvage a bit of their dignity by fast-forwarding to it. Then they find themselves keeping meticulous accounting of the facts in order to determine whether continuing to bear with their mates conforms neatly to "good common sense."

When only predictions of future probabilities guide you, it seems completely logical to conclude, *"We cannot possibly belong together. It would be foolish for us to go on."* When you are ruled by common sense alone, it will eventually demand that you think of your marriage as a mathematical calculation with but one invariable answer. Because the kind of unconditional commitment required in marriage can never be fully explained by common sense. If it could you would never ask or trust an invisible God to sustain what, try as you might, you cannot sustain on your own. Marriage is the deliberate act of giving your life to love another person based on your most *uncommon* sense.

What in your marriage looks bleakest to you? What appears to be teetering on the brink of collapse? It will not do to deny that there are such areas. You are certain to fall victim to dangers that you stubbornly denounce the existence of. Every honest survey of marriage reveals some signs of weakness in some area. And some of these will undoubtedly appear to be forewarning the death of your union. But will you resist the urge to pronounce it dead when in fact it may only be dormant?

The headlines were full of the story of the television celebrity's husband who was caught on video in a compromising position with another woman. The star was devastated when she discovered that her mate's affair had gone on for a very long time. Many months later, after the couple had reportedly reconciled and their marriage was back on track, a TV interviewer asked her how she had managed to remain in the marriage after such a horrible public scandal. "At the time didn't you think it would have made better sense to dump him and go on with your life?" The celebrity explained that when her husband's philandering came to light, logic had indeed suggested that her marriage was dead; but that it was something other than logic that convinced her to treat it as if it were terminally ill and had a tiny chance of being miraculously cured. She said she willed herself to act each day (and hold her husband accountable to act) as if their marriage could and would survive and eventually flourish again. Though she must have felt tremendously foolish at the time, she kept using good *un*common sense.

To uphold a vow of uncommon sense is to take all that you know, within yourselves and between you, then add to that the elements of faith. It will mean intentionally going beyond the limits of your rational conclusions. At times it will mean looking past what your mate has said or done to what he could not bring himself to say and was not quite able to do. To love her at the seat of her deepest needs when she is at her most unlovable, when your common sense says she doesn't deserve it, and when you feel as if you have nothing more to offer her.

Uncommon sense is to act as if what may at first appear to be irreversible circumstances are not at all. Uncommon sense must never be confused with reckless stupidity. Faith and the invisible realities of miracles, are not simply positive thinking or foolish presumption. Recognize that if your marriage is to emulate the way that you are loved by God, you must admit that is a kind of love that defies natural laws. It is not earned but freely given. It is offered with no condition of reciprocity.

That is the clearest mark of the difference between common and uncommon sense. The former is always directed at what will keep you from losing, or investing for negligible returns. The latter will direct you to give or withhold, abide or depart, speak or be silent, embrace or rebuke, according to what causes the one you love to gain. Uncommon sense is lavish and unreserved in its expression. It is not blind to present reality, but does not insist that present realities alone can predict the future. Uncommon sense springs from your abiding confidence, not merely in your own grit and determination but in God's limitless ability to resurrect what we would logically but prematurely call hopeless.

For the health of your marriage, have you ever had to do something difficult even though at first it did not seem logical to do so? Have you ever been surprised to discover that it was a wise choice?

The Vow of Resilience

Our long-cherished and well-established idea of how marriage is "supposed to be" is subject to unexpected modifications.

WHEN HE FOUND HER, she was sitting on a stone at the edge of the marshlands. Adam sat next to her. A gentle, almost imperceptible breeze swayed the reeds that normally stood sturdily at attention. "We were going to build our home on these banks, remember?" Eve recalled somewhat sadly. "Um-hmm," said Adam. "And you were going to have a garden pond just over there. I remember." "Adam, we dreamed and planned so many wonderful things for our life together. What happened to them?" Adam chuckled and took her hands in his. "Work, children, responsibilities, the passing of time . . . who knows? Now I only dream of sleeping!" The Man could see that his wife was in no mood for jesting. "Let go of them, Eve. We have so much more than we planned on. The house we would have built here would not have been big enough for our sons and us. And though many of our dreams never came to pass, I never dreamed back then that I would grow to love you in the way I do now." As Eve turned to look into the face of her husband the giant stalks of the pampas grass parted to make way for The Creator's entrance. Over the constant fluttering of the geese's comings and goings, God spoke to Adam and Eve about The Vow of Resilience.

I fully understand how difficult it is for you to accept the fact that nothing lasts forever. I've watched you, and even heard you sigh and your shoulders droop when you see lilies, once pulsing with life, bow to the soil and die. You rise and go on, but you have never gotten comfortable with anything that once held vibrant life ever giving way to death. Make a vow to each other, before Me, to mourn the dead things of your union only long enough to be grateful that they were. Then look with new eyes at the tomorrow I have prepared for you. How sad it would be if your

marriage never changed, never grew, never stretched, never outlived today. That, my darlings, is real death. That is a death I will never permit you to endure as long as you both shall live and love as I do.

In marriage, we are especially averse to accepting—much less embracing—the demise of things we hold dear. Feelings shift. Goals change. Opportunities slip away. Plans and intentions, your health, your material possessions, will eventually fade. No matter how pleasant or painful, your life is measured in seasons and cycles; what you may have believed would last forever is soon found to have been temporal. What you thought would be constant, instead ebbs and flows as the waves of the sea.

Those who resent the very idea of change try to freeze *now* into icy permanence. They hold the one they love hostage, requiring that their mates keep doing, saying, and being, exactly the same as in the past. They yearn for the familiar, even when the new and unfamiliar promises greater rewards.

Some of your oldest and most cherished hopes and dreams concerning your marriage will be fulfilled, but in a downscaled version of the original. Some of your surest expectations of how married life is "supposed to be" will at first seem within reach, only to end up eluding your grasp. Some of your long-held secret heart's desires may never see the light of day. You can choose to live in a permanent state of regret or you can acknowledge the demise of old expectations and desires and you can, with resilience, rise and embrace the new possibilities that have replaced them.

After years of working with every kind of couple you could imagine, I still marvel at the exceptional ones who can admit the disappointment of life's inevitable losses and still pick up and move from there into the unexpected blessings that have emerged to replace them. Those rare, resilient men and women form my gallery of unforgettable heroes:

- The resilient couple that suffered the unexpected loss of their "dream business," and in the process discovered a new level of mutual support and unconditional commitment they had not known existed.
- The resilient couple that moved from regret over their unexpected infertility into their dream of parenting—by adopting.
- The resilient couple that moved beyond an unexpected family tragedy that interrupted their peaceful early retirement to assume the rearing of their young grandchildren.
- The couple who, after enjoying years of a mutually satisfying sex life, experienced unexpected illness and went on to discover nonsexual ways to express their profound love for each other.

These husbands and wives, and many like them, have embraced a real-life vow of resilience, and in doing so have found that they cannot cling forever to yesterday's joys or its sorrows.

Embrace the change and the inevitable losses that will occur throughout your marriage. Mourn your unexpected losses; anticipate the unexpected gains. What you once had, did, hoped for, or required may have been glorious; but you must look forward to what surprising blessings will follow.

Fearful resistance declares, "I will not accept this. I cannot adjust to this." But you can and you must. The miracle of marriage is not in your ability to keep the unexpected, the unwanted, and the unplanned from happening. Instead, both of you must stay committed to each other and the life you share as you adapt to these inevitable transitions.

You are in a perpetual process of repair and renewal. Shifts and changes are the only real constant. There are greater strengths you are yet to gain, greater challenges, and more wisdom and fearlessness with which to meet them.

What do you personally find most challenging about accepting unwelcome circumstances and moving on? What are you now willing to do about it?

The Vow of Rest

When everything else becomes more urgent than your own renewal, you and all that matters most to you will begin a slow but steady decline. Much of what you need in order to even keep caring about your marriage at all can only be accessed in stillness.

EVE HEARD ADAM CALLING her, but she would not answer. She continued to feed their son. He would be asleep soon and she'd be able to get to the work in the garden and repair the oil press, and tend to a hundred other things that demanded her attention. Adam entered in a huff, annoyed. "Didn't you hear me calling?" "What is it now, Adam?" Eve snapped. "What is it that you cannot find though it's right under your nose? What is it that you cannot manage without my help? Or were you wanting to tell me how difficult I have been lately? Or how moody or lazy or selfish, or what, Adam?" Eve shrieked in exasperation. Adam was taken aback by the cold force of her tone. He opened his mouth to object, to declare his outrage, to point out the inappropriateness of her remarks. But no words came out. Instead, he found himself walking calmly over to Eve and gathering her to his chest. Within seconds she began to weep. Deep, weary, moaning sobs that had built up over many exhausting days. As Adam held his wife, The Creator held them both and began to tell them of The Vow of Rest.

Rest is not an option. It is a necessity. What will it profit you to gain all the world's good and all of each other's affections but lose yourself in utter fatigue. Regularly come to quiet reflection and complete rest that I may revitalize your body and your spirit.

Sometimes it is only that you have not rested. Fatigue has sapped your body of its strength and has now seeped into your mind and spirit. It is not because you've been taken for granted or because the two of you have forever lost the love you once had. It is not because you are a mismatched set, or two that can never become one. Appearances to the contrary, God has not left you alone, and your world is not on the verge of crumbling. It could simply be that you are tired; and when you are tired this long, you begin to see your marriage in darker, bleaker hues.

Keeping the daily commitments of marriage requires tremendous physical and spiritual endurance. You are ill prepared to operate on that level without sufficient rest. When burdens and demands are heavy upon you, you are tempted to look upon stillness, momentary inactivity, and slumber as selfish indulgences that you simply cannot afford at this time. For the sake of your own well-being and the health of your marriage, rest is a necessity that you can ill afford *not* to indulge.

When everything else becomes more urgent than your own inner renewal, you and everything that matters most to you will begin to operate at a chronic state of decline. Fatigue is a dark, isolated place where marriage's most threatening forces grow and flourish. Bitterness, indifference, suspicion, impatience, isolation, and every kind of temptation will threaten to undermine your intimacy and your appreciation of the life you share together.

Soon every area of your marriage operates at less than capacity. Your capacity to work at it is reduced. Your capacity to feel is diminished. Your interest in maintaining your relationship, setting goals, understanding, protecting, and caring—all fall victim to self-neglect.

Over the weeks leading up to our family's move to a new city, stress and the fatigue it brings became major threats to our marriage. Our energies were spent on an endless stream of highly demanding logistical details. We were nearly consumed by weeks of sixteen- to eighteen-hour days. Soon, in our exhaustion, we lost sight of each other. Evenings out together ceased, as did our usual flirtations with each other, leisurely conversations, our nightly prayer time, and even lovemaking. We were simply too tired to be anything other than vaguely irritated by each other's presence.

We withdrew to our separate corners and began to buy into the idea that we weren't *really* as loved and cared about by our mate as we had thought. Then the inevitable chain of flawed logic that plagues the weary set in: *"Why,"* we questioned, *"should I go through all this trouble to move away with somebody who cares so little about me?"*

During this emotionally detached season we found that we had to take the vacation we had long since booked at a popular spa resort or we'd lose the money we paid for it. Though we didn't cherish the thought of being with each other for a week at the height of our "crisis," the booking couldn't be rescheduled. We took the red-eye to Puerto Vallarta.

Once there we slept, we swam, we overdosed on massages and mud baths. After a few days of rest we were able to recognize that fatigue had us seeing in our marriage problems that really weren't there. I shudder to think what might have happened had we made a life-changing decision when we were so tired.

You have everything you need to be refreshed and renewed. Only you mustn't expect to find it as you continue at your frantic, overloaded pace. You will not be able to receive it fully if your mind and heart are divided in their focus. Much of it will only be accessed in complete stillness. Otherwise the demands of living your life in concert with each other will deplete your emotional, spiritual, and physical reserves. Then your way of loving each other will become mindless habit.

It will mean letting go of some of your emergencies. They are never finished. You must stop in the midst of them, fearlessly interrupting the fulfillment of tasks and obligations you considered urgent. For a time your mate and others may be inconvenienced and annoyed by your sudden halt. Suffer it to be so. In quiet repose you will find the peace that is available only to those who are willing to

cease their striving and relax in the assurance that only God holds the
world together.

What are you letting get in the way of devoting adequate
time to your own rest and renewal? How did rest
become a lower priority in your life?

The Vow of Relentless Pursuit

Your highest aim is not merely to honor and cherish your mate, nor even to grow old together, prosperously and contentedly. The defining objective of your marriage is, and must ever remain, to profoundly experience God's extraordinary love and commitment, and to imitate it in your marriage.

THE SUN SEEMED TO TAKE its time rising, but each second of its leisurely ascent brought a fresh new wash of color over every sleeping and waking thing in The Garden. Adam and Eve stood barefoot atop the northern hill, which was blanketed with golden poppies. The Creator watched The First Couple silently drink in the stunning view He had spread before them. There was no need for Him to utter a word to them. He knew that every tree and flower, every bird and scurrying beast, every smell and sound and sight would declare His glory and bring to their remembrance all the vows that He had taught them. The Creator waited for each memory to sink in and bear its blessed fruit in them. He was confident that they would strive to nourish their devotion to each other with the overflow of all the love and affection He had lavished upon them. He watched as emotion began to overtake them. Every wonderful thing He had placed around them became a reflection of every wonderful thing He had placed in them and that had been shared between them. Eve looked up at her husband with bright, wet eyes. Instinctively, Adam drew close and kissed her. "You are my heart's desire, wife," he whispered in her ear. At that moment the Creator unveiled Himself in the warm glow of the risen sun. He knew their petition even before they voiced it. "Yes, I will surely stand as Witness to your vows this day, My beloved," He assured them. So there on a great hill overlooking the splendor of Eden, The First Husband and First Wife stood before God and made to each other an outrageous commitment to hold forever true The Vow of Relentless Pursuit.

Everything about your marriage is not what you had in mind. At times you see clearly more of what you expected to see little of, and in some ways, very little of what you actually envisioned more of. So many of

your expectations have fallen short or failed to materialize. This is not nearly what you expected marriage to be. You must not be intimidated by the disparity between what is visible in your marriage and what is hoped for, yet unseen. All is not as it appears. You know only what is behind you and immediately before you, not what may be just around the next bend. My plans for you extend beyond what you presently see. I alone hold your tomorrows. With each rising of the sun I bring you ever closer to laying hold to My kind of marriage, the kind that far exceeds your earthbound dreams. It can and will be yours if you will put aside your fears, your pride, and your tendency toward self-reliance and instead put your total faith—however small or great—in Me, the God Who keeps every promise. The stroke of My brush, the mysteries of My will, and the timing by which I move will not always make complete sense to you. Though it will not always be easy, yours is to continue relentlessly in your determination to keep offering each other the kind of unconditional, invincible commitment that I extend to you.

The highest aim of marriage is not to honor or cherish your mate. It is not to grow old and prosperous together. It is not that you become a better person or help make the world a better place. The defining objective of your marriage is, and must ever remain, to know God's extraordinary love and commitment to you and to imitate its commitment in loving each other. It is simply to regard your mate as God regards you, and to love him or her with no strings attached.

It is responding out of grace and compassion even when it hurts to do so, or when your mate is clearly undeserving of it. It is seeking true justice, not just self-justification. It is actively seeking reconciliation and accord, not just peaceful detachment. Most important, it is in being content with *whom* you married, though the person isn't always exactly *what* you wanted. It is loving someone as much as you love yourself, even though you do not always know how to show that you do.

Occasionally your efforts will fail, but the Source of your strength never will. You promised to love, honor, and cherish each other until death parts you. Even when you break that promise, the God Who is relentless in His love for you is well able to pick up the slack. He is using you to make your marriage much more than it is, and using your marriage to make you much more than you ever thought you could be.

Are you willing, by the grace of God, to make and keep these 48 vows, from this day forward, until death separates you?

Afterword

In the final days of writing this book I had to take a late-night flight east that included a layover in Las Vegas. As I sat waiting for my connecting flight I began brainstorming for just the right way to end this book. What final words would inspire you, the reader, to make and keep the forty-eight vows you've encountered here. Mindful of the maxim "a picture is worth a thousand words," I groped for one perfect, unforgettable image that could galvanize your commitment to live what you have learned in these pages.

My thoughts were so scattered, so forgettable that after several minutes, I gave up to indulge in one of my favorite pastimes: airport people-watching.

A plane had just landed and a stream of passengers noisily flooded into the gate area. Many of the new arrivals appeared to be married couples. One ultra-affectionate couple (they had an unmistakable newlywed air) emerged from the jet-way holding hands and smiling broadly, then stopped spontaneously for a long passionate kiss. The man excitedly exclaimed "Let the good times roll!" Equally enthused, she squealed in agreement. They were obviously in love and thrilled about the delights awaiting them in this capital of fun and games. They set off to retrieve their bags. Just as they passed me she spied the ladies' room and lightheartedly announced that she needed "to make a pit stop." She asked him to wait for her there. Put off by the threat of a minute's delay, he urged her to wait until they got to their hotel. Instantly a look of impatience and annoyance swept over both their faces. They squared off to glare and sigh in each other's direction. Eventually she turned and headed into the rest room. He scowled dramatically and stomped off to the baggage claim, leaving her behind. The opening scene of these newlyweds' love story had started on a high note but ended in mutual frustration. So much for passion.

In the meantime, among the other arriving passengers was a couple who without trying had caught the attention of almost everyone around them. They were a senior couple apparently married for a long time and by now accustomed to living life in the seasoned familiarity of each other's company. What made them so noticeable was that due to some physical disability she walked with a slow, unsteady gait, requiring that she hold her husband's elbow for support. He balanced her feeble steps with the steady strength of his own. There was one other noticeable fact: he, sporting large-framed dark glasses and a red-tipped cane, was obviously blind. He relied upon her vision to navigate them, as much as she relied upon his agility to propel them.

There were no showy romantic displays of affection between them, only the simple, breathtaking image of a husband and wife who knew what unique strengths the other possessed and what they lacked. They both benefited from each other's strengths; but refused to let their individual liabilities stand in the way of their forward movement—together.

Mesmerized, I watched them for several minutes as they slowly made their way up the long corridor and out of sight. Then it hit me like a ton of bricks. It was shortly before midnight near arrival gate 6 at the Las Vegas airport that I witnessed, in the silent passage of this extraordinary couple, a living picture of the grace and acceptance that define outrageous commitment. Here my unforgettable image of the kind of selflessness and steely perseverance that make a marriage indestructible.

It's what I pray for and vow to work toward in my own marriage. And it is my greatest hope for yours.

Acknowledgments

A picture of *An Outrageous Commitment* should appear in the dictionary next to the word *collaboration*. I owe a tremendous debt of gratitude to my wife, Aladrian, my children, Corinn, Christina, and Cory; my agent, Marlene Connor-Lynch; my editor, Kelli Martin; and my assistants, Kalif Durham and Yvonne Miller; my church, Faith Fellowship; and to Michelle Jones for her invaluable editorial contributions. Thank you all for accompanying me on this book's incredible journey.

An Outrageous Commitment was inspired by the many men and women throughout the country who have experienced powerful transformations in their relationships by applying these principles.

For more information about Dr. Ronn Elmore, his speaking engagements, and helpful resources for building an indestructible marriage and an extraordinary life, visit

www.DrRonn.com

and

www.harpercollins.com